HYDROPONICS

12 EASY AND AFFORDABLE WAYS TO BUILD YOUR OWN HYDROPONIC SYSTEM

RICHARD BRAY

Published by *Monkey Publishing*

Edited by *Lily Marlene Booth*

Cover Design by *Diogo Lando*

Printed by *Amazon*

ISBN (Print): 978-1-7292-0907-3
ASIN (eBook): B07JKPY7S8

1st Edition, published in 2018

© 2018 by Monkey Publishing

Monkey Publishing

Lerchenstrasse 111

22767 Hamburg

Germany

All rights reserved, including the right to reproduce this book or portions thereof in any form whatsoever except for brief quotations in critical reviews or articles, without the prior written permission of the publisher.

YOUR FREE BONUS

As a small token of thanks for buying this book, I am offering a free bonus gift to my readers.

Hydroponics is a new and innovative way of growing plants, but that doesn't mean it's difficult. As with anything new, there will be a learning curve at the beginning. To accelerate your learning, the free bonus offers additional tips for successful hydroponic gardening practices.

In this bonus package, you will learn:

- How to set and control the climate for your plants
- 9 tips on how to regulate water temperature easily
- How to keep the oxygen and nutritional levels well balanced
- Simple ways to keep your roots healthy and thriving
- 15- step formula to raise your seeds successfully

You can download the free gift here:

https://DIYhydroponics.gr8.com

RICHARD BRAY

CONTENTS

CHAPTER 1: THE BASICS OF HYDROPONICS.................................... 15

    A SIMPLE INTRODUCTION... 16

CHAPTER 2: TYPES OF HYDROPONIC SYSTEMS................................ 18

    OVERVIEW OF DIFFERENT SYSTEMS.. 19
        Drip System.. 19
        Ebb and Flow... 22
        Nutrient Film Technique.. 25
        Water Culture.. 26
        Aeroponics... 29
        Wick Irrigation.. 31

CHAPTER 3: BUILD YOUR OWN HYDROPONIC SYSTEM.................... 32

    HOW TO SET UP A WICKING SYSTEM... 33
        The Four (or Five) Main Components of a Wicking System.......... 33
        How to Make a Wicking Hydroponic System............................. 37
        How to Turn a Soda Bottle Into a Wicking Hydroponic System..... 39

    HOW TO SET UP A WATER CULTURE HYDROPONIC SYSTEM......... 42
        The Five Main Components of a Water Culture System............... 42
        Recirculating Water Culture System... 46
        Deep Water Culture System... 48
        How to Convert an Aquarium Into a Water Culture System......... 48
        How to Turn a 5-Gallon Bucket Into a Deep Water Culture (DWC) Hydroponic System.. 53

    HOW TO SET UP AN EBB AND FLOW HYDROPONIC SYSTEM......... 55
        The Seven Main Components of an Ebb and Flow System........... 56
        How to Make an Ebb and Flow System out of Plastic Storage Containers (Stacked Method) 63

    HOW TO SET UP A DRIP HYDROPONIC SYSTEM........................... 68
        The Seven Main Components of a Drip System......................... 69
        How to Build a Recovery Drip System with 5-Gallon Buckets........ 73

    HOW TO SET UP A NUTRIENT FILM TECHNIQUE SYSTEM.............. 81
        The Five Main Components of an NFT System.......................... 82
        How to Build an NFT Hydroponic System with PVC Pipes......... 86

HOW TO SET UP AN AEROPONIC HYDROPONIC SYSTEM.............	93
The Seven Main Components of an Aeroponic System.............	95
How to Build a 5-Gallon Bucket Aeroponic System................	97
CHAPTER 4: GROWING MEDIUMS, NUTRIENTS & LIGHTING...........	**102**
GROWING MEDIUMS..	103
Rockwool..	103
Coco Coir...	104
Expanded Clay Pellets...	105
Perlite..	105
Vermiculite..	106
Gravel..	106
Starter Plugs/Cubes...	106
NUTRIENTS...	109
Nutrients You Need for Your Hydroponic System.............	112
How To Add Nutrients to Your Hydroponic System..........	112
Testing the pH...	113
Flushing...	115
Optional Additives for the Plants.................................	115
LIGHTING...	119
Fluorescent Lights..	120
Compact Fluorescent Bulbs...	120
High-Intensity Discharge (HID) Lights.........................	120
LED Lights...	121
CHAPTER 5: HOW TO MAINTAIN A HYDROPONIC SYSTEM............	**122**
CLEANLINESS..	123
NUTRIENT SOLUTION...	123
WATERING..	123
RESERVOIR TEMPERATURE...	124
HUMIDITY..	125
INSPECT THE EQUIPMENT..	126
LOOK AT YOUR PLANTS!...	126
TAKE NOTES!..	127
CHANGE ONE THING AT A TIME.......................................	127
CHAPTER 6: POTENTIAL PROBLEMS AND HOW TO OVERCOME THEM....	**128**
PESTS..	129
Thrips..	129
Aphids...	130
Spider Mites..	131

Fungus Gnats...	131
White Flies..	132
How to Combat Pests...	132
DISEASES...	133
Root Rot...	134
Gray Mold..	134
Powdery Mildew..	134
Downy Mildew..	135
Iron Deficiency..	135
Calcium Deficiency..	135
Rust..	135
How to Combat Diseases...	136
SYSTEM PROBLEMS...	136
Algae Bloom...	136
Nutrient Deficiency	138
Clogged System...	142
GETTING STARTED...	143
APPENDIX I – GLOSSARY...	**145**
APPENDIX II – IDEAL PH LEVEL FOR YOUR HYDROPONIC PLANTS	**155**

GRAPHIC PREVIEW

Convert an Aquarium into a Water Culture System (Excerpt)

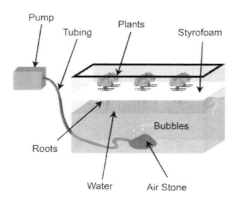

HYDROPONICS

Build an NFT Hydroponic System with PVC Pipes (Excerpt)

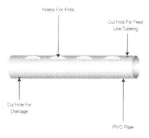

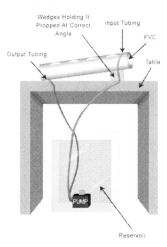

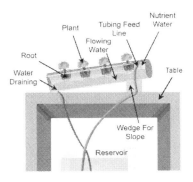

RICHARD BRAY

Build a Recovery Drip System with 5-Gallon Buckets (Excerpt)

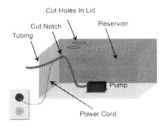

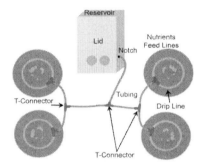

Top View Of Buckets

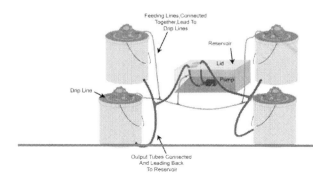

Why You Should Read This Book

Hydroponics is a rewarding method of gardening and one that I hope you will enjoy as much as I do. The best thing about a hydroponic set-up is that you don't need a patch of land in order to grow amazing fruits and vegetables. In many cases, you'll need no more room than the space of a small table. A hydroponic system can be as simple as you like or as complex as you can imagine.

Hydroponics is a new and innovative way of growing vegetables, but that doesn't mean it's difficult. As with anything new, there will be a learning curve at the beginning. However, once you get the hang of it, I think you'll agree it isn't complicated at all.

This book will take you through the six main hydroponic systems, explaining each one in detail, and give you step by step instructions on how to create and maintain your own hydroponic system. If you don't want to rely on ready-made kits for your hydroponic garden and you want to feel the pleasure of creating your own system from scratch, this book is for you. DIY systems provide you with satisfaction in seeing tremendous results from something you build with your own hands. They are a rewarding, cost-effective approach to the creation of your own homegrown food. This book provides different designs to fit everyone's needs. From easy-to-apply methods for small plants, such as using a soda bottle to build your own Wick System, to more advanced instructions for larger systems such as building a Nutrient Film Technique System with PVC pipes.

And this is just the beginning. Once you've got your feet wet (so to say!), you can expand your systems and making them as complex as you like. Growing vegetables the hydroponic way can be quite easy and lots of fun.

CHAPTER 1: THE BASICS OF HYDROPONICS

Before we go into detail on how to build and maintain your own hydroponic system, I'd like to give you an overview of the basics of hydroponic gardening. Take this as the starting point for a journey that will provide bountiful crops all year-round.

A simple Introduction

You don't need to be a farmer to begin your own hydroponic garden. Nor do you need acres of land. All you need is a willingness to learn different ways of cultivating plants. Hydroponics has been around for at least 500 years. The first book on the subject was published by Francis Bacon in the 17th century. Since then, there have been numerous innovations in the field, but the basics remain the same.

This method of farming can be used both indoors and outside. All you need is a basic understanding of how to set up your hydroponics growing system(s), and you're off!

What you are about to create, with the help of this hydroponic guide is a method of growing vegetables, herbs and fruit at home without the use of soil. The roots will instead rely on a nutritionally enriched liquid. They are nourished in water, supplemented with liquid nutrients. You can use mediums, such as perlite and vermiculite, or even rockwool and clay pellets, but more on that later.

There are many ways to create a hydroponic system. You can either buy a kit or you can assemble a system from scratch with your own equipment. Ready-made kits are a great option if you want to save time and effort and jump straight into the growing process. They also won't require too much explanation, as the process is fairly simple once you begin. So, while we'll cover ready-made kits, much of the book will be devoted to DIY hydroponics. DIY hydroponics is easier and more rewarding than you might expect, and this book will give you all you need to know to begin your hydroponic journey.

CHAPTER 2: TYPES OF HYDROPONIC SYSTEMS

Before we get started with instruction plans, we should have a look at different hydroponic systems. In this chapter, we will look at six different ways of growing crops hydroponically. Once armed with this knowledge, it will allow you to assess which system is best for your own personal situation.

Of course, you may want to run more than one system, depending on the space available and what types of plants you wish to grow. First, let's go over the growing techniques:

OVERVIEW OF DIFFERENT SYSTEMS

DRIP SYSTEM

The Drip System is one of the most popular hydroponic systems. It is employed world-wide both for personal and commercial use.

• Basically, water and nutrients are slow-dripped into the growing tray which houses the plant's roots.

• This system is ideal for plants with larger roots and for growing in hotter climates where water is sparse.

• As with most hydroponic systems, the drip system requires two tanks. One tank is the growing tray which houses the plant roots in a suitable growing medium. Beneath this is the reservoir tank, which stores water and nutrients and contains the pumps.

• There are two pumps in this system. One delivers nutrient-rich water to the growing tray from the main reservoir. This can be controlled by a timer switch. The second pump aerates the water in the main reservoir with the aid of an air stone.

• •With the help of the air pump, air stones deliver to the tank many small bubbles that are filled with oxygen. While an air pump and tube can function without the use of an air stone at the end of the line, growers prefer air stones, which help diffuse the oxygen better than the larger tube can without it.

• The drip line is the tube which supplies nutrient-rich water to the plants. Liquid drips out of the emitters, which control the amount of water each plant receives. The water lands on the growing media and drains down to feed the roots. Each plant needs its own drip line.

• Gravity drains any excess liquid into the reservoir where it can be recycled. It is important to keep the growing medium damp. It should not be allowed to become either soaked through or completely dry.

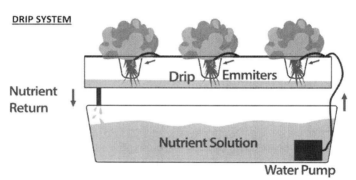

Illus. 1 - Drip System Set-Up

The Drip Method can perform in one of two ways. It can be either recirculating/recovery or non-recirculating/non-recovery. The names of the systems are self-explanatory. They refer to whether or not the water is recycled.

- *Recirculating/recovery* systems are often used by home growers to keep costs down. The nutrient-rich water is not always used up by the plants. Rather than draining away, it returns to the reservoir tank via an overflow pipe. With this method, any water that collects in the bottom of the growing tray is recirculated through the system. The grower needs to check the pH levels of this system periodically. This is because nutrients will tend to become watered down in the recovery process. Also, the grower will need to top up the reservoir tank with nutritional solution from time to time.

- *Non-recirculating/non-recovery* is more popular when using the Drip System on a larger scale. With this method, excess water runs off as waste. It requires an extra piece of equipment called a Cycle Timer. This will add fresh nutrients into the main reservoir tank at timed intervals. Every now and then the growing media will need flushing with fresh water to prevent mineral build-up and algae growth.

EBB AND FLOW

- Also known as the Flood and Drain System.

- Popular with home growers.

- The medium that contains the roots is flooded at timed intervals. A flow of nutrient-enriched water is provided by a pump from the main reservoir, which again, sits below the grow tray. Water then returns to the main reservoir through a gravity-powered overflow pipe.

Here are some of the variations of the Ebb and Flow method:

- **Tray Container**

In this method, plants sit on a layer of growing medium in a large tray. Nutrient-enriched water is pumped through a tube from the bottom reservoir into the growing tray. When the water reaches a certain level, the overflow returns to the reservoir below. One disadvantage of this system is that it can be difficult to remove individual plants as the roots can become entwined.

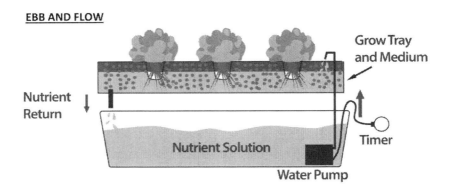

Illus. 2 – Ebb And Flow Set-Up

• **Separate Containers**

Plants sit in separate pots, each containing a growing medium. The pots are placed in a large tray which fills with water. The rest of the procedure is the same as the tray method, with water draining back down to the reservoir. One advantage of this system is that individual plants can be removed easily because they are in separate pots.

• **Surge**

The main difference between the surge method and other variations of Ebb and Flow is that the reservoir tank does not need to be below the growing tray. There are still two tanks: the reservoir and the surge tank. The surge tank, which is at the same level as the growing pots, feeds the nutrient-enriched water via a pump. The growing pots are connected to the surge tank via pipes that sit below the water line.

The principle is that the water in the surge tank is at the same level as it is in the growing pots. When the water in the surge tank reaches a certain level, a pump is activated. This returns the water to the main tank. As the water in the surge tank drops, so does the water in the growing pots. This system is more expensive to construct as there are more parts required.

The size of your water pump depends on the design of your hydroponic system. It is advisable to get a bigger pump than you actually think you'll need, because you can always reduce the water flow but not vice versa. You can use simple submersible fountain and pond pumps for your hydroponic system.

NUTRIENT FILM TECHNIQUE

• Ideal for small, quick-growing plants.

• The reservoir tank sits underneath the growing compartments and contains nutrient-enriched water. This water is pumped to separate grow channels.

• The growing compartments are usually gullies or tubes that allow the water to flow through. Plants sit in a basket on the tray with their roots suspended through a hole. This method allows the roots to access the nutritional flow of water in the bottom of the gully.

• Nutrient-enriched water is pumped up through a tube. It enters one end of a growing channel which sits on an angle. Water flows down the slope and returns through a waste pipe situated at the other end of the gullies. The roots act like a wick and soak up the liquid.

• •This method requires accurate measurement of flow rate and a correct slant angle in order to be effective.

• The flow is constant, so the pump must be active at all times.

• Roots are more exposed in this system. Because of this, it is important to monitor humidity and temperature levels. If you don't, the roots could dry out or become waterlogged, which could result in the loss of the entire crop.

- You need to watch out for roots clogging the system and blocking the water flow.

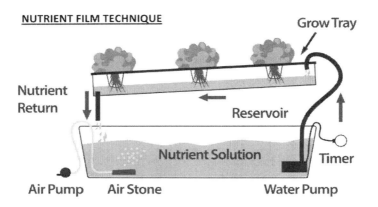

Illus. 3 – Nutrient Film Technique Set-Up

WATER CULTURE

- Popular for commercial farming as it is an inexpensive method for large-scale usage. It is equally as popular with the smaller homesteaders because there are low initial setup costs and it can be as small or large as the available space.

- Only uses one tank. The main tank houses both the nutritional water and the plants. Some growers use interconnected growing tanks and circulate the water between them. However, this requires a pump.

• Plants sit with their roots suspended in the water via hanging baskets. Alternately, holes can be cut into the lid of the reservoir tank. The plant sits in the lid with its roots suspended in the water through the holes.

• No water pump is required because plants sit in the nutritional water continuously.

• You'll need to top up the tank with water and nutrients well as they are used up by the plants.

• A system of aeration is needed to ensure the plants receive the necessary oxygen.

WATER CULTURE

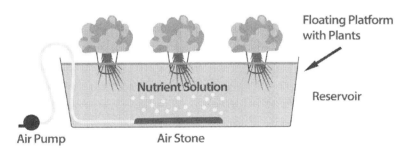

Illus. 4 – Water Culture Set-Up

Here are some options you have for oxygenating the water:

• **Air Pump**

Pumps the oxygen into an air stone that sits on the bottom of the tank. Air bubbles rise into the water for the roots.

• **Waterfall**

Water cascades into the tank at force, agitating and aerating the water in the reservoir.

• **Recirculating Water**

Similar to the Ebb and Flow System. The water never completely drains out and the roots are always submerged. Water is pumped into the growing pots, ensuring the plants receive sufficient oxygen to thrive. Once the water reaches a certain level, it is returned to the reservoir via an overflow.

AEROPONICS

• Would you believe that this is fast becoming popular in modern restaurants? It allows them to grow their own products and display them in growing towers. Aeroponics is known as vertical farming and is one of the leading hydroponic systems in commercial industries. It's a great method for any indoor gardener.

• Only one tank is required for aeroponic systems.

• Roots hang down through holes in the lid of the tank. The difference between this system and the water culture method is that the roots are not suspended in water. Instead, they remain exposed to the air. This makes for an oxygen rich atmosphere.

• The plants do not need any growing medium.

• The tank has nutrients and water at the bottom and a pump for water delivery.

• The roots are sprayed by water and nutrients in short bursts from a sprinkler underneath. This requires that the sprinkling system be set up inside the tank.

- The growing tank is the most important element of this system. When set up correctly, it retains humidity and allows for a constant flow of fresh oxygen.

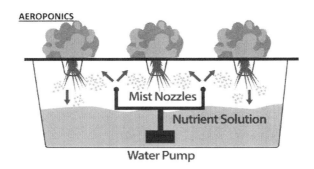

Illus. 5 – Aeroponics Set-Up

- The tank should be airtight so pests cannot get inside. This will protect the exposed roots.

- If the pump stops for any reason, the roots can dry up quickly and the entire crop may be lost.

- This spray method can be set up in different ways. Each system will alter the size of the droplets in the sprinkling: High Pressure, Low Pressure and Foggers. The higher the pressure, the larger the droplets. The Fogger has the smallest droplets and provides water in the form of a mist.

WICK IRRIGATION

• This is the simplest method. It is also the most cost-effective means of growing plants hydroponically.

• Requires no use of pump or electricity.

• Only one tank is needed. The plant containers sit above the reservoir that contains the nutrients and water. A wick(s) hangs down and drops into the water solution. It soaks up the nutritional water, which in turn dampens the plant medium, to feed the roots.

• •The system can be as simple as one plant pot that sits above the reservoir. Its wick hangs down and enters through a hole. Larger systems could include several plants in a tray with multiple wicks dangling into the solution.

• The growing medium will need flushing periodically to stop algae or mineral build up.

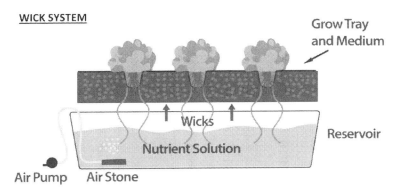

Illus. 6 – Wick System Set-Up

CHAPTER 3: BUILD YOUR OWN HYDROPONIC SYSTEM

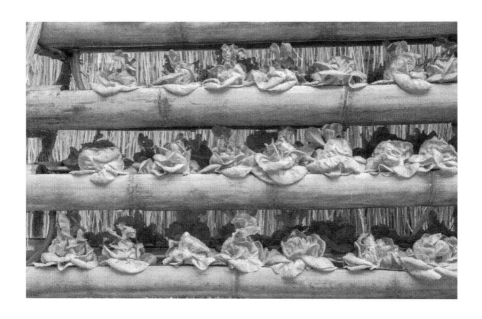

Now that you understand the basics of the six types of hydroponic systems, let's learn more about building them. The next six sections of this book go into specifics about each system. The components of each system are explained in detail along with variations and options. This guide will help you determine and create the ideal system for your growing needs. In each section, there is a step-by-step guide, with detailed explanation and illustrations of how to build the system along with a list of all the needed tools and materials.

HOW TO SET UP A WICKING SYSTEM

The Wicking System is the simplest hydroponic system and the easiest to set up. It takes very little planning or in-depth engineering to construct. It's the best method for beginners and also makes a great hands-on project for children. The wicking system is categorized as a passive system because it contains few moving parts. No special machinery or equipment, such as pumps or motors, are needed to keep the system operational.

Because of their basic design, Wicking Systems work best for plants that don't require a lot of monitoring or water and that are generally easier to grow. Herbs and vegetables like lettuce and other leafy greens are excellent choices for this method. Tomatoes and other fruiting vegetables are not ideal, as they require a great deal of water.

THE FOUR (OR FIVE) MAIN COMPONENTS OF A WICKING SYSTEM

- Wick
- Grow Tray

- Growing Medium
- Reservoir
- Aeration System (optional)

The Wick

The centerpiece of this hydroponic set-up, and the source of its name, is the wick. The term wicking refers to a material's ability to absorb and transport liquid through a porous surface. Some common examples of wicking are the way in which a paper towel soaks up spilled juice from the floor and how fabrics soak up the sweat from your skin. It works because water molecules like to cling to one another in close cohesion. They also stick to other surfaces in the same way. The ability of a wick or tube to transport water is known as capillary action. In this case, the wicking material absorbs water and nutrients, transporting them to the roots of your plants.

A wick can be made of or re-purposed from a variety of different materials. Fibrous rope, rayon rope, yarn, felt, nylon rope, and strips of fabric from old clothing or blankets all make excellent wicks. Two things to consider when choosing a wicking material are the rate at which it absorbs water and its ability to withstand rotting. To test the wicking ability of your chosen material, or to test the wicking of several different materials against one another, place the ends of each in a container of dyed water and monitor how far the colored water travels up the cloth in an hour.

The shorter your wick, the quicker it will deliver water and nutrients to your plants. It is best to situate your plants right above the reservoir if possible. Each plant will have at least one wick, possibly two, depending on what you're growing.

The Grow Tray

In this method, you plant seeds in a grow tray which holds the growing medium. It can be just one pot or a tray that holds several plants, depending on how big a system you want to build and what you are growing.

The Growing Medium

Since the water will be delivered at a slow speed by the wicking material, it's best to choose a growing medium that absorbs and holds water very well. Ideal choices for this include vermiculite, perlite, and coconut coir.

Another good choice is a soilless potting mix. A soilless potting mix is composed primarily of sphagnum peat moss. It is inexpensive, lightweight, holds water plentifully and at the same time, drains well. Soilless potting mixes often blend peat moss with coconut coir, bark, or vermiculite.

Whichever growing medium you decide to use, it is important to flush it out every few weeks with fresh water to prevent a build-up of nutrients. If the nutrients are allowed to accumulate to high concentrations, they can become toxic to your plants.

The Reservoir

Water and nutrients are stored in the reservoir. The bottom of the wick is suspended in the nutrient-enriched water of the reservoir and transports it to your plants. The reservoir doesn't have to be complicated or fancy. However, it's preferable that the container be dark in color because light will encourage algae growth.

If you are using a container that is see-through, either paint it a dark color to prevent light from entering or create a shade to place around it. The second option is preferable, especially if you make it removable. This allows you to keep it in place during the growing cycles and remove it when checking water and nutrient levels.

It is important to keep the reservoir filled, as the wicks are more effective when the water has less distance to travel. If the reservoir gets low, then the water has further to travel and your plants won't be receiving the correct level of hydration. Lower hydration levels can slow the growth of your plants.

Please see the Water Culture section to determine the recommended size for your reservoir.

Optional Aeration Device

To refine your Wicking Hydroponic garden and make it more efficient, you may choose to include an aeration system. Aeration systems ensure that the water has enough oxygen in it to promote healthy plant growth. Your plants will still receive oxygen from the air without such a system, but they can absorb oxygen more easily from their roots. By aerating the water, you'll promote quick and healthy plant growth. You can make an effective and inexpensive aeration system with no more than an aquarium air stone and pump.

HOW TO MAKE A WICKING HYDROPONIC SYSTEM

This design is for a basic system with only a few plants. You can expand on it as far as you like. If you want to grow many plants, simply get a large grow tray and large reservoir. For just one plant, use a pot and a small reservoir. A great way to start is to build a small system at first to let you get a feel for the process. Once you are comfortable with that, you can expand the system or build a larger one.

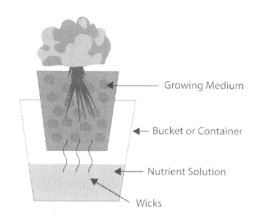

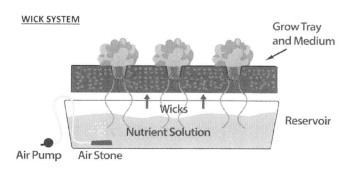

Illus. 7 – Small and Large Wick System Set-Up

What You Will Need:
- Grow tray – it can be a tray for several plants or a pot for one plant
- Growing medium
- Two strips of wicking material per plant
- Reservoir
- Nutrient solution
- Aeration system (Optional) [air pump, air stone, tubing]

Assembly:

1. Fill the grow tray or pot with the growing medium.

2. Arrange the wicks in the growing medium so they hang down far enough to reach the reservoir. If your grow tray does not have holes in it, you will need to cut some to fit the wicks.

3. Space your seedlings out in the growing medium.

4. Fill your reservoir with water and nutrients.

5. Arrange the grow tray on top of the reservoir so that the wicks dip into the nutrient water solution.

6. Congratulations, you've made a wicking hydroponic system!

7. If you want to add the oxygen system, connect the tubing to the air stone. Place the air stone in the reservoir. Attach the other end of the tubing to the air pump (the pump DOES NOT go in the water). Turn on the pump and make sure the air stone is producing bubbles.

HOW TO TURN A LITER SODA BOTTLE INTO A WICKING HYDROPONIC SYSTEM

There are several different methods you can use to build your own system. The simplest, and a favorite in classrooms around the country, is the soda bottle method.

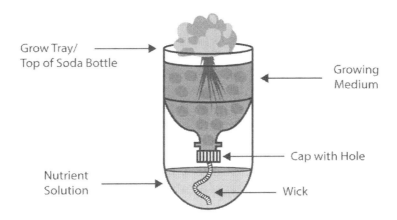

Illus. 8 – Soda Bottle Wick System

What You Will Need:
- 1 clean plastic 2-liter soda bottle, with cap
- Scissors
- Rubber bands
- Duct Tape
- Wicking material
- Growing medium
- Nutrient solution

Assembly:

1. Cut the soda bottle 8" from the top.

2. Cover the cut edges of the bottle with duct tape to prevent slippage after assembly.

3. Cut a hole in the cap large enough to thread the wicking material through. Thread material into the hole so you have half the length of the wick on each side.

4. Mix the water and nutrient solution (according to package directions). Fill the base of the soda bottle to 4" from the bottom. You may need to add more or reduce the amount, depending on how far the inverted bottle goes down.

5. Invert the top of the bottle and fill with your growing medium, making sure the wick is weaved and stretched out through it.

6. Plant your seedling in the growing medium.

7. Fit the bottle top, cap side down, into the bottom half of the bottle. Make sure the wick is free to rest in the nutrient solution.

8. The bottle cap should be above the water level with the wick dangling down into the nutrients.

Caring For Your Plants In A Wicking System

- When the nutrient-enriched water solution gets low, replace it entirely with a new mix of water and nutrients.

- Flush the growing medium with fresh water every two weeks to prevent harmful nutrient buildup.

HOW TO SET UP A WATER CULTURE HYDROPONIC SYSTEM

The Water Culture system of hydroponics is commonly referred to as the purest hydroponic system, as it is entirely water-based. There is no growing medium used to hold the plants in place, and the roots of the plant are continuously immersed in aerated water.

The main benefit of using this type of system is that it is relatively inexpensive and easy to set up. Also, there are few moving parts that could be prone to break down. The downside is that because it is a small system, nutrient concentrations and water levels can fluctuate widely. There is a strong possibility of over- or under-compensating. A power outage or pump failure can also be an issue. If the pump is not continuously supplying oxygen, the plants can 'drown'.

The disadvantages of this system can be overcome by careful monitoring and maintenance. You'll want to check the system daily to make sure that everything is working properly.

THE FIVE MAIN COMPONENTS OF A WATER CULTURE SYSTEM

- Net Pot
- Reservoir
- Lid/Grow Tray
- Growing Medium
- Oxygen Pump System (Pump, Tubing, Air Stone)

Net Pot

A net pot may sound a bit strange, but the name is self-explanatory. It is a small round plastic basket with holes in it that make it look like hard netting. The basket weave holds the plant so it doesn't fall into the reservoir, while the roots grow out through the holes. Net pots come in a variety of sizes to accommodate different sizes of plants and systems. Don't forget, the root system will become larger as your plants grow. You'll want to select a size that will accommodate this growth.

Reservoir

The reservoir holds the water and nutrient solution and it won't need to be very deep. The ideal depth depends on what plants you are growing. For example, lettuce will flourish with a reservoir that holds four to six inches of water. To determine the appropriate depth, consider the length of the root system at full growth.

A common rookie mistake is to use a reservoir that is too small. It can be hard to imagine that such a little seed will grow to produce such a huge root system. Your plants will grow quickly with this system and the roots can outgrow a small container before you realize it. Switching containers halfway through the growing process can be both expensive and an unnecessary hassle. This can also damage your plants, so it's best to plan the correct setup from the beginning.

To make sure you select a reservoir large enough for your needs, consider what you plant in each pot and how many pots you'll set up in the reservoir. In the section on the raft method below, you'll see that these systems can contain quite a few plants. Consider the size of your plants at full growth, and then use this rule of thumb to determine reservoir size:

- For small plants, supply a minimum of a ½ gallon of water per plant
- For medium plants, supply a minimum of 1 ½ gallons of water per plant
- For large plants, supply a minimum of 2 ½ gallons of water, per plant

It is always best to err on the side of caution, so don't be worried about using a much larger container than you think you need. In fact, you may wish to choose a container double the expected size. Make sure to keep it filled with enough water to cover the roots, regardless of how much water is required per plant.

If you use a raft-type lid and a large container, it's helpful to mark the 1-, 2-, and 5- gallons points and so forth on the inside of the container with a permanent marker. This will help you to determine how much water you need to refill the reservoir as the levels drop. It will also make it easy to monitor how fast your plants are absorbing water.

If you use a bucket or another large container with a fitted lid, make sure to fill it high enough to keep the roots submerged. If you use a see-through reservoir, make sure to cover it with a removable shade. Any light entering your reservoir will break down the nutrient solution and encourage algae growth.

Lid/Grow Tray

The lid is designed to cradle the net pot so it doesn't fall into the nutrient solution. It is usually a flat surface with a hole cut in the center. The hole should be large enough to fit the bottom half of the net pot, yet not so large that it allows the entire net pot to slip all the way through. It is then secured firmly to the reservoir to keep it in place.

Alternatively, you can use a floating raft. Styrofoam is the most common medium used to create a raft since it will float on top of the water reservoir and provide a buffer between the water and the upper portion of the plant. Multiple holes can be cut in the Styrofoam, angled slightly, and somewhat smaller than the size of the net pots. The goal is to suspend the net pots securely in place and prevent them from sliding through.

Growing Medium

In the Water Culture System, no soil is needed. However, it is sometimes necessary to use a material to keep the seedling plant secure in the net pot while it grows. There are several choices for this. Rockwool is an excellent choice. It comes in cubes specially designed for hydroponic gardening. You can also use wood chips, packing peanuts (Styrofoam), vermiculite, perlite, coconut fiber, expanded clay pellets (grow rocks), rice hulls, or pumice.

Make sure the pieces of material are large enough that they won't slip through the holes in your net pot and fall into the reservoir. Also, it's preferable to choose a material that is resistant to mold or fungus. Fungus can damage the roots of your plants and endanger the crop.

Air Pump/Air Hose/Air Stone

The air pump, hose, and stone work together to create an aeration system to oxygenate your nutrient solution. In a Water Culture System, the more air bubbles, the better. The bubbles need to make direct contact with the root systems to deliver oxygen. The water in the reservoir should look almost like it's boiling.

An aquarium air pump and air stone will work fine for this system. They are easy to find at pet stores or online. The pump is connected to the stone via the tubing. The pump drives air through the tube into the porous air stone. Small bubbles then stream upwards from the stone.

A soaker hose can be used in place of the air stone. Soaker hoses will produce small bubbles. These have a higher surface area by volume, delivering more oxygen for the same volume of air pumped through the medium. Put simply, the smaller the air bubbles, the better.

RECIRCULATING WATER CULTURE SYSTEM

Recirculating water culture systems connect several growing reservoirs to one central tank. You may wish, for example, to use five large buckets or storage containers. One will act as the controller bucket, while the other four contain plants in net pots. The buckets can then be linked in series, connected to one another with intake hoses and overflow tubes. The controller bucket will contain a large pump to drive the water in the system. Pond or fountain pumps are an ideal choice. The pump sends the water into the first bucket in the series, which then overflows into the next, and so on. The final bucket overflows back into the controller bucket to recirculate the nutrient solution.

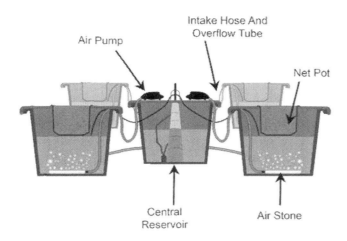

Illus. 9 – Recirculating Water Culture System

This method is often used by large commercial growers. The advantage of this approach is that growers only need to check water and nutrient levels of the controller container. However, the water is not aerated as completely as it is in other systems. This results in slower plant growth.

DEEP WATER CULTURE SYSTEM

This term is often used as if it is completely different from a Water Culture System. However, the only difference is that in a deep water culture system (DWC), the water in the reservoir is deeper than 8".

HOW TO CONVERT AN AQUARIUM INTO A WATER CULTURE SYSTEM

What You Will Need:
- An airtight glass aquarium

- Material for a light shield (aluminum or cardboard work great)
    - If you would like to monitor root growth, make your light shield removable.
- Floating platform –1½" to 2" thick layers of Styrofoam are ideal. Cut the raft to fit loosely inside the reservoir.

- Net pots to hold the plants. You could also use a small plastic cup with tapered sides. Simply cut holes to allow the roots to grow through.

- Growing medium of choice (Expanded clay pebbles are recommended to keep seedlings in place)

- Aeration system (air pump, air stone, tubing to connect them)

- Nutrients (see the chapter on choosing nutrient solutions for your hydroponic garden)

- pH test kit (Optional yet highly recommended. They are inexpensive and absolutely worth the cost.)

Assembly:

1. Cut holes in your Styrofoam floating platform to fit your net pots. Make sure the holes are smaller than the net pots so they don't fall through. The bottom of the cups should hang just below the Styrofoam.

2. Add growing medium to each of the pots. If the medium begins to fall out of the holes, you can place a small piece of cloth over the holes first. Set aside.

3. Fill the reservoir/aquarium with water. You can always add or remove water if necessary.

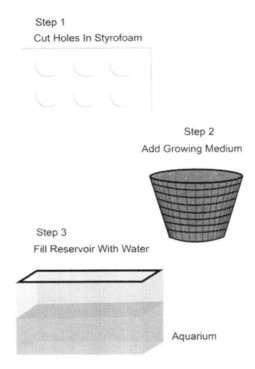

Illus. 10 – Aquarium Water Culture System Set-Up

4. Mix nutrients as per package instructions and add to the water.

5. Test your pH and adjust the nutrients accordingly. Different plants require a different pH. To check different pH requirements for plants see Appendix II - Hydroponic Plants pH

6. Attach tubing to the air stone and place it in the water.

7. Attach the free end of the tubing to the air pump (the air pump DOES NOT go in the water) and situate it on the side of the reservoir.

8. Plug in the pump and make sure that the air stone is producing bubbles.

9. Arrange the floating platform on top of the water.

10. Put your seedlings in the net pots, secured gently by the growing medium.

11. Put each pot in its hole in the platform. The bottom of the pots (i.e. the plant's roots) should be submerged in the water. Be careful not to submerge the stem.

12. Congratulations, you've created a water-based hydroponic system!

Side View

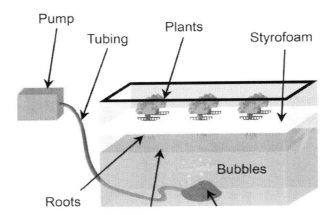

Illus. 11 – Side View: Aquarium Water Culture Set-Up

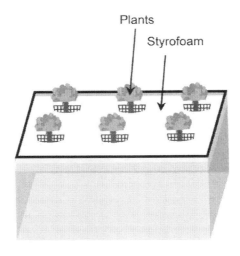

Illus. 12 – Top View: Aquarium Water Culture System

Caring For Your Plants In A Water Culture System:

• Add water only (no nutrients!) when the plants have absorbed half of the solution.

• Check your pH levels and adjust only if needed

• The second time the plants have absorbed half the solution in the reservoir (approximately every 1-2 weeks, depending on what you're growing), it is time to refresh the nutrient solution. Drain the reservoir completely and blend a fresh batch of nutrients and water.

HOW TO TURN A 5-GALLON BUCKET INTO A DEEP WATER CULTURE (DWC) HYDROPONIC SYSTEM

What You Will Need:
- Five-gallon bucket with lid
- Net pot or another container with tapered sides and holes cut in it for roots to grow through
- Aeration system (air pump, air stone, tubing to connect them)
- Growing medium
- Nutrients
- pH test kit

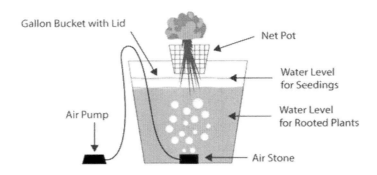

Illus. 13 – 5-Gallon Bucket Water Culture System Set-Up

Assembly:

Follow the instructions listed above for the aquarium set-up. The only difference is that instead of cutting a hole for your net pot in Styrofoam, you will be cutting a hole in the lid of your 5-gallon bucket. Remember to make the hole smaller than the pot so the pot doesn't slip through.

HOW TO SET UP AN EBB AND FLOW HYDROPONIC SYSTEM

Though this system looks complicated on paper, once you set it up and see it in action, you'll see that it's one of the simplest designs. Ebb and flow systems are easy to manage and can be adapted to fit any space, as large or as small as you like, and any shape you desire. You'll need a timer and a fill/drain overflow fitting kit, but these are easy to find at any hardware store. You'll also need a drill to put holes in the growing container and reservoir. This system is quite versatile, making it a popular choice for home gardeners.

The basic mechanics of an Ebb and Flow System are as follows: Plants are housed on a grow tray which is attached with tubing to a reservoir. The pump is on a timer and floods the grow tray with nutrient-solution several times a day. The flooding time is typically a minute, after which time the pump turns off. Gravity drains the water back into the reservoir through the pump. An overflow drain is also set up to ensure all water returns to the reservoir.

In this method, the plant roots are flooded for several short periods during the day. The rest of the time, they'll be out of the water and exposed to oxygen. This way, both oxygen and nutrient absorption are optimized promoting strong plant growth.

THE SEVEN MAIN COMPONENTS OF AN EBB AND FLOW SYSTEM

- Grow Tray
- Reservoir
- Growing Medium
- Fill/Drain Overflow Fitting Kit
- Pump
- Tubing
- Timer

Grow Tray & Reservoir

These are listed together because, in most designs of this type of system, the grow tray and reservoir are connected. The size of one will determine the size of the other. In the stacked container design, the grow tray will fit snugly into the reservoir. Alternately, the grow tray can sit on a separate table. For this design, the size of growing tray and reservoir do not need to be matched so closely. Regardless of which setup you use, the grow tray must be above the reservoir for the pump to operate correctly and create the ebb and flow.

There are two basic types of grow tray arrangement. The first uses a single grow tray which has all the plants in one place without separation. The entire tray gets flooded with the nutrient solution at the same time. The benefit of this design is that it is easier to assemble. The downside is that the plants can't be moved around easily. This system can be set up using the stacked-container arrangement or with a separate table to set the grow tray on.

The second type of grow tray system uses individual growing containers for each plant. These containers are placed in a tray which gets flooded with nutrient solution. This design can support many plants and the grow container can become very heavy. Because of this, it's best to support the grow container by placing it on a table rather than using the stacked container design.

When planning the size of your grow tray, consider the space that you have available and how many plants you want to grow. Reservoir size will be dependent upon space and upon how many plants you want to water. The key is to ensure there is enough water to flood the grow tray. Smaller reservoirs also require more frequent nutrient top-ups. As the plants grow larger, they will use up water and nutrients more quickly. A small reservoir will do the job while plants are still small, but it's better to overestimate reservoir size than to underestimate. Your plants may grow very large, and faster than you may expect.

Please see the Water Culture section to determine the ideal size for your reservoir.

The stacked container arrangement is commonly used for an Ebb and Flow System because it makes the best use of space. It consists of one large plastic container as a reservoir (for example, a 20-gallon storage bin), and a smaller container of the same length and width, yet shorter in height, to serve as the grow tray.

The grow tray must fit snugly on top of the reservoir without falling into it. It needs to have a lesser depth than the reservoir, so when the tray sits on top, it leaves plenty of empty space between the bottom of the tray and the bottom of the reservoir. This empty space between them will contain the nutrient water.

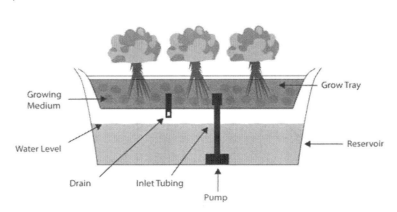

Illus. 14 – Ebb and Flow System – Stacked Container

Alternately, the grow tray can sit on top of the reservoir instead of nestled inside of it. Either way, grow tray and reservoir containers must work in conjunction with one another.

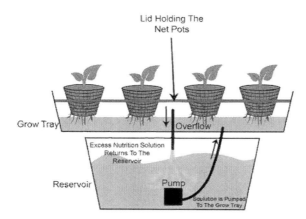

Illus. 15 – Ebb and Flow System – Reservoir Sits on Top

Another popular way to set up this system is to place the growing tray on a table and the reservoir on the floor below. Longer tubing is used to connect the two. It generally takes up more space to set it up like this. If you are setting up a large system though, the table set-up is a good option. The table will support the weight of more plants or larger plants, and it makes it easy to inspect the plants as they grow.

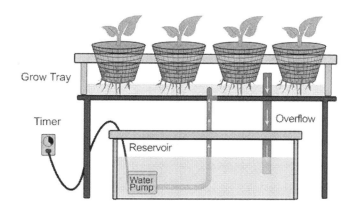

Illus. 16 – Ebb and Flow System - Grow Tray Sits on Table

An opaque reservoir container is recommended. This will make it more challenging to check the water level, but it will shield the water in the reservoir from light. If you use a transparent container, you will be able to see the water level, but you'll also need to cover the sides so the light doesn't encourage algae growth. If you opt for a transparent container, it's best to use a removable covering so you can both shield it from light and easily check the water level.

Growing Medium

The grow tray or grow containers need to be filled with a medium to support the plants. Options include expanded clay pebbles (Hydroton), granulated Rockwool, vermiculite, perlite, coconut fiber, and gravel. Each medium has different absorptive capacities, so you'll need to adjust your flooding times accordingly.

A common choice is expanded clay pebbles. Clay pebbles provide great support and plant roots can easily grow through them. They are the preferred option if you place the plants directly in the grow tray instead of in individual containers. On their own, clay pebbles don't hold much water, so you'll need to flood your tray approximately every 2 hours.

Clay pebbles can be mixed 50/50 with diatomite to soak the roots for longer per flooding period. Diatomite is more absorbent than clay pebbles, so you will need fewer irrigation periods per day.

Another suggestion is a 50/50 mix of coconut fiber and perlite, with two inches of clay pebbles lining the bottom. This combination offers aeration, moisture retention, and a secure foundation for the seedlings. By lining the bottom of the tray or container with clay pebbles, you'll prevent the other medium from getting washed away when the grow tray is flooded.

Your growing medium should be allowed to dry out well in-between flooding periods. Early in the growing process, this will allow your roots to absorb plenty of oxygen and reduce the risk of root rot. Near harvest time, it will encourage your plants to flower. Plants in constantly wet medium will produce lots of green foliage instead of large fruits or vegetables.

Fill/Drain Overflow Fitting Kit

These kits are readily available online or at your local home and garden store. They are inexpensive and consist of two hard plastic threaded pieces attached to a grow tray. They come in several sizes and the size of your tubing will need to match your fittings. Many companies sell inexpensive Ebb and Flow fittings sets.

The smaller piece of the kit is for the inlet. This allows water to be pumped up into the grow tray. The longer piece is for the overflow tube. It has slits around the threaded top that allow the water to flow back into the reservoir. The overflow drain is extremely important. Without it, if your pump malfunctions, water could overflow out of your grow tray.

Pump

The pump should be strong enough to deliver the water from the reservoir to the grow tray but not so strong that it turns your water into a fountain. Pump specifications will indicate how high they will pump. This is measured in HEAD, so if a pump is rated at 3 feet of HEAD, then it will pump 3 feet. If the pump only has a PSI (pounds per square inch) rating, you'll need to multiply that number by 2.31 to get the HEAD. A good rule of thumb is to get a pump with a HEAD rating at least double of what you need.

Tubing

The size of your tubing should match the size of your Fill/Drain fittings and your pump fitting. How much you need will depend on your system setup and the distance between your reservoir and grow tray. Clear irrigation tubing is recommended.

Timer

There are two timer options: segmental (or mechanical) and digital.

A segmental timer is set to go off at specific intervals. For example, it can be set for every 20 minutes, every 6 hours, or whatever span of time you want between flooding periods. The benefits of the segmental timer over a digital one are lower costs and easier setup. The downsides are that they are less accurate than digital timers, some of them have a loud ticking noise that people find irritating, and their settings can get thrown off if you accidentally bump into them. Interruptions in power will also upset the programming. The timer shuts off when the power goes off and turns back on when the power returns, without accounting for the time it wasn't working. This can severely mess up your cycles.

With a digital timer, you can set the specific flooding time(s) each day. You can set it, for example, for every morning at 8 a.m. and every evening at 10 p.m. Digital timers are more precise than segmental ones, however, there are some downsides. They are much more expensive and can be a challenge to set up. Despite this, they have a number of advantages. Digital timers usually have a backup battery, so power outages won't interfere with the timing of your cycles. You can also set digital timers in ways that aren't possible with segmental timers. They can be set to do things on specific days of the week or combinations of days, at specific times and for very precise amounts of time. Finally, digital timers will allow you to set your flood times to smaller intervals. Given the increased reliability and greater control over irrigation times, digital timers are preferable.

A general purpose 15-amp timer is ideal. 10-amp timers often burn out so it's worth spending a few extra bucks for the 15-amp version. You'll save more cash in the long run. An indoor/outdoor timer is also recommended because they are grounded and safer to use around water.

As with anything dealing with electricity, please exercise caution when setting up your timers. It is important to avoid overloading sockets or power outputs. This can have serious consequences. Please pay close attention to the amps!

HOW TO MAKE AN EBB AND FLOW SYSTEM OUT OF PLASTIC STORAGE CONTAINERS (STACKED METHOD)

Choose a spot for your Ebb and Flow System that gets an appropriate amount of light for your growing plants. Make sure you have access to an electrical outlet. You must set it on a level surface so the water can drain through the pump efficiently. If the surface is not level, you will have water pooling at the bottom of your grow tray. Roots can rot if they are left suspended in water without enough oxygen.

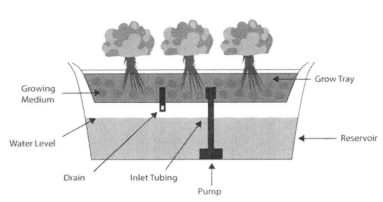

Illus. 17 – Ebb and Flow System – Stacked Container

What You Will Need:
- 16-20 gallon storage tote bin, preferably opaque or dark colored.
- 30qt clear storage tote bin, or a similar size that will fit snugly on top of the larger container
- Timer
- Clay pebbles or medium of choice
- Containers for plants (ideal size will depend on what you are growing and how many will fit in your grow tray)
- Irrigation tubing, 1/2" inner diameter, approximately 18"
- Submersible pond pump with 1/2" fittings

- Fill and drain fitting set, 1/2"
- Power drill with appropriate fittings to drill holes for fill and drain fitting set and for overflow tubing.
- Wooden dowel or flat stick longer than the height of your tallest container that you can write on.
- Nutrients
- Plants

Assembly:

1. Drill two holes in the bottom of the smaller container. These are for your inlet (water going into the grow tray) and overflow (water draining out). The inlet hole will need to accommodate your fill fitting so measure accordingly. The overflow hole is where the tubing goes, so make it a little bit smaller than your tubing so it can fit securely. If you make it too big, you will need to get wider tubing.

2. Attach the fill fitting set to your inlet hole.

3. Cut a piece of hose to link the inlet fitting to the pump outlet. The length of tubing needs to be long enough for the pump to sit at the bottom of the reservoir while the grow tray is on top. This will take some testing; you may need to adjust it to get it right. Cut the tubing longer than you need, and then trim off small pieces until it fits nicely. You may have to secure the tubing on both sides with a zip tie. Make sure the fit is secure at both ends.

4. Seat the pump at the bottom of your reservoir.

5. Cut a piece of hose for your overflow. It needs to be long enough to be above your anticipated water flood height in the grow tray and still reach into the reservoir without touching the water. Fit the tubing into the overflow hole. Attach the overflow fitting to the top of the tubing so it is in the grow tray.

6. Run the cord from your pump between the two stacked containers so the plug is on the outside of your system.

7. Fill your reservoir 2 gallons at a time. After each addition, measure the increase in water level with a wooden dowel, marking each increment. This will let you know how much nutrient-water your plants are using and how much more you will need to add.

8. Fill with a total of 10 gallons of water.

9. Add the nutrients as per package instructions.

10. Fill the plant containers with your growing medium.

11. Plant the seedlings in your containers, arranging the growing medium snugly around them to keep them in place.

12. Place the containers in the grow tray and fit the tray on top of the reservoir, being careful to keep the pump plug cord out.

13. Set up your timer and pump. They should be set to flood 3 times a day, 15 minutes per cycle.

Caring For Your Plants In An Ebb And Flow System:

- While your plants are getting used to their new system, it is recommended that you water them from the top for a few days so the roots don't dry out.

- Inspect daily to make sure all the water is being drained properly.

- Check frequently for blockages in the overflow pipe and tubing.

- Change out nutrient-water weekly.

HOW TO SET UP A DRIP HYDROPONIC SYSTEM

The Drip System is one of the most popular design choices for hydroponic growers. It is extremely effective and uses water more efficiently than many other systems. Also, because the nutrient-water is dripped right at the plant's roots, plant growth is rapid and yields are higher.

A Drip System consists of a grow tray, a reservoir and a drip line positioned at the base of the plants. The pump is hooked up to a timer. When the pump is active, it will drip nutrient-water onto each plant. There are two types of Drip System setup, Recovery Drip System and Non-Recovery Drip System. A Recovery Drip System collects the nutrient-water runoff and recycles it back to the reservoir for reuse. A Non-Recovery Drip System does not collect or reuse the water.

The benefit of a Recovery Drip System is that you will use less water and nutrients over time. The challenge of this system is that it requires you to pay close attention to the concentration of nutrients in your water. As the water is reused, the nutrients will decrease in strength. You'll need to check pH and nutrient concentration frequently.

Non-Recovery Drip Systems are used mostly by commercial growers. The downside of this system is that it is less economical. However, growers can time watering cycles to the second. When the plants are watered, they get only as much as the growing medium can accommodate for each watering. The plants are watered more frequently and for precise amounts of time, so you can make sure the watering cycles exactly fit your plants' needs. A major benefit of this system is that you won't need to monitor the nutrient-water concentration so closely. However, you will need to change the water in the reservoir weekly to keep it from becoming stagnant or building up an excess of minerals.

Drip systems are preferable for larger plants. They provide plenty of growing medium for large root systems and you won't need huge amounts of water to flood the system. Cucumbers, tomatoes, peas, zucchini, and pumpkins are some popular choices.

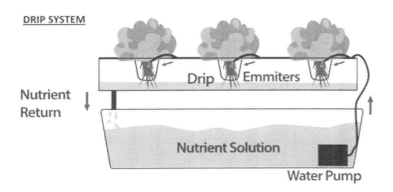

Illus. 18 – Drip System Set-Up

THE SEVEN MAIN COMPONENTS OF A DRIP SYSTEM

- Grow Containers

- Reservoir
- Growing Medium
- Tubing
- Submersible Pump
- Timer
- Drip Stakes (optional)

Grow Containers

There are many ways to set up a Drip System. The grow container you use will depend on how you choose to set it up. It's important to remember that this system doesn't already have holes in it, so you will need to make your own holes.

A common design choice is a 5-gallon bucket or several buckets connected together. Another option is potting specifically designed for a Drip System set-up, these are called Dutch Buckets or Bato Buckets and are available at most hydroponic stores.

Most growers prefer individual containers because they allow you to remove one plant without disturbing the rest. However, a single long grow tray can also be used. The benefit of using a grow tray is that it is slightly easier to set up. Instead of drilling holes in every single container, you only have to make holes in one. And, if you would like a simple, space-saving setup, you can get a grow tray that sits on top of your reservoir. This eliminates the need to find or build a table that will hold your individual containers.

For this system, it is important that your grow containers can hold a good amount of growing medium and that holes can be cut or drilled in the bottom of the buckets.

Reservoir

The reservoir in this design is very simple. It needs to hold enough nutrient enriched water to feed the plants for a week, or for however long you have decided to make your watering schedule. If you are building a recycling system, you will be conserving water and won't have to worry so much about water loss.

The reservoir can sit to the side of your grow containers or tray. If you are using a grow tray, you can situate it on top of your reservoir to conserve space. If you go down this route, keep your reservoir size in mind when purchasing your grow tray.

Medium

A few popular choices for medium are coco chips, perlite, vermiculite, clay pebbles, and rockwool. Mediums are often mixed for optimum performance. Rockwool and coco chips are highly absorbent and can lead to over-saturation if the drippers run too frequently. Clay pebbles are ideal for a Drip System because they don't absorb much nutrient-water and are unlikely to be over-saturated. When using clay pebbles it's almost impossible to over-irrigate.

Tubing

Some Drip System designs use all the same size tubing and others use different-sized tubing for the drip lines and water delivery line. In the end, system design is up to you. If you use the same diameter for both lines, you can save a few bucks on startup materials.

For large systems, it may be helpful to use larger-diameter tubing for the delivery line to reduce stress on the pump. The majority of systems use 1/2" vinyl tubing for the delivery line and 1/4" tubing for the drip lines. The size of your tubing should match your pump outlet and tube connectors.

Submersible Pump

Please see the information on pumps for Ebb and Flow Systems.

Timer

Please see information on timers for Ebb and Flow Systems.

Drip Stakes

Drip Stakes are plastic pegs that look similar to tent stakes. They attach to a drip line and carry the nutrient solution into the growing medium. The benefit of using drip stakes is that nutrients and water penetrate the medium instead of landing on top of it. This means that less nutrients will be lost through surface evaporation. It's ideal to use two stakes per plant in case one gets clogged. The downside to using drip stakes is that if they malfunction or become clogged, it's hard to notice before the plants are in trouble.

To clean your drip stakes, soak them in a bucket of vinegar solution. It's best to have backup drip stakes on hand so that when one is being cleaned, another is available to replace it. An alternative to using drip stakes is to use a ring of perforated tubing to deliver nutrient solution to your plants.

HOW TO BUILD A RECOVERY DRIP SYSTEM WITH 5-GALLON BUCKETS

Before getting started, plan out how you will arrange your buckets. The amount of T-connectors and tubing required will depend on your layout. Make sure all connectors, tubing, and fittings are the same size. The reservoir should be at least 6 inches below your buckets. A good way of setting this up is to place the buckets on a sturdy table with the reservoir beneath it. Make sure your setup is within reach of an electrical outlet.

What You Will Need:
- 4 5-gallon buckets
- 4 bulkhead fittings for your tubing
- Filter material
- Medium-sized rocks to fill the bottom ¼ of each bucket (washed and sanitized)
- Black or blue vinyl tubing
- Submersible pump
- 30-gallon storage tote bin
- Growing medium [I suggest 1 compressed block coco chips –

uncompressed, it equates to 2 cubic feet and is enough for all 4 buckets]
- 8-10 T-connectors to fit your tubing
- Timer (preferably 15 amp)
- Nutrients
- Plants
- Drill to make holes in the bottom of plastic buckets
- Paperclips and a candle or lighter

Assembly:

1. Trace the size of your bulkhead fitting onto the bottom of each of your 5-gallon buckets and cut a hole. The placement of the hole should be close to the edge of the bucket yet not so close that you will have a problem threading the fitting in it. It's ideal to make it about 1-inch from the edge.

- Be careful not to make the hole too big. If it leaks, you've got a problem. It should be just wide enough to fit the threaded end without leaving a gap.

2. Insert the fitting into the hole and tighten it. The rubber gasket should be on the outside of the bucket.

3. Cut your filter material and secure it around the fitting inside the bucket. This is to prevent growing medium or other debris from clogging up lines.

4. Fill the bottom of the buckets with the rocks.

5. Fill each bucket with the growing medium.

6. Cut a small notch in the rim of each bucket to hold the tubing securely in place.

7. On top of the growing medium, make a circle with your tubing and use the T-connectors to connect the two ends. Do this with all 4 buckets.

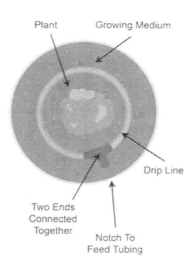

Illus. 18 – Recovery Drip System – Growing Bucket Set-Up

8. Heat the end of a paperclip with a candle or lighter. Use the

heated end to create holes in the drip lines. Make sure your holes face down towards the growing medium.

9. Run tubing from each bucket to the top of the reservoir.

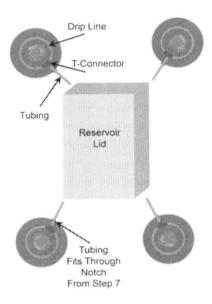

Illus. 19 – Recovery Drip System – Tubing Alignment

10. Cut a notch in the lid of your reservoir bucket large enough to fit the power cord and tubing for your pump. Cut two holes in the lid of the reservoir.

11. Place your pump in the bottom of the reservoir and arrange the power cord so it goes through the notch.

12. Cut a length of hose to run from the pump to your bucket tubing. Attach one end to the pump. This is the feed line that delivers nutrient solution to the drip lines.

13. Run the feed line through the notch hole in the lid of your reservoir.

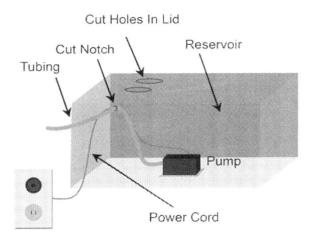

Illus. 20 – Recovery Drip System – Reservoir Set-Up

14. Attach a T-connector at the end of the feed line.

15. Cut two pieces of hose to run from either end of the T-connector.

16. Attach a T-connector to the ends of each of the hoses. You

should now have 4 open connections that all feed back to the reservoir. Hose length for all steps will depend on how you have set up your buckets and how far apart they are.

17. Insert tubing from your buckets into each of the ends of the T-connectors.

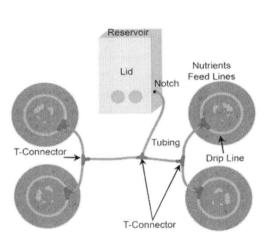

Illus. 21 – Recovery Drip System – Drip Lines Set-Up

18. Cut 4 pieces of tubing to attach to the fittings at the bottom of each bucket. With a T-connector, attach the tubing from two buckets together. Cut another length of tubing to run from this T-connector to one of the holes in the reservoir lid. This is how your nutrient-water will drain back to the reservoir. Do the same with the other

two buckets, with the tubing going through a hole in the reservoir lid.

> o The exact lengths of your tubing will depend on your system setup. You will connect the bottom of 2 buckets together with tubing attached to a T-connector and then run a length of tubing from the T-connector through the hole in the reservoir lid.

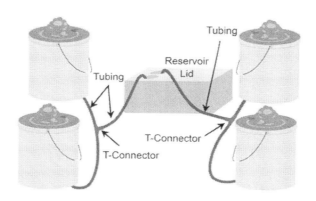

Illus. 22 – Recovery Drip System – Output Tube Set-Up

19. Set up your timer. The frequency will depend on what you're growing. A common setup is three times a day for 15 minutes each session.

20. Fill your reservoir with water and add the appropriate amount of nutrients as per package directions.

21. Plant your seedlings in the growing medium.
22. Run your system and watch your plants thrive!

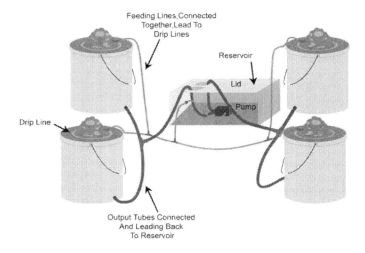

Illus. 23 – Recovery Drip System – Complete Set-Up

Caring For Your Plants In A Drip System:

• Regularly inspect the drip lines and tubing for clogs. Any material blocking the flow of water can have quick and harsh consequences.

• Check your timer and pumps on a regular basis. Any interruptions or malfunctions will cause your plants to be deprived of nutrients.

• Check your reservoir level regularly. You'll need to refill the tank more frequently if you don't recycle the water.

• Test pH and nutrient levels. If you recirculate the water, the nutrient concentration will drop before you need to change the water.

HOW TO SET UP A NUTRIENT FILM TECHNIQUE SYSTEM

Nutrient Film Systems work with gravity to send a thin film of nutrient solution continuously flowing over the exposed plant roots. The benefit of this technique is that the plants receive a constant flow of nutrients. The downside is that any disruption in the system, for even the smallest amount of time, can cause catastrophic failure for the entire crop.

In an NFT System, nutrient-enriched water is pumped from the reservoir through tubing to the gullies or channels which hold the plants. The water flows down the sloped sides of the channels, wetting the plant's roots. The plants are suspended above the water at the top of the channels with the roots hanging down. The shallow film of nutrient-water flows by and feeds the roots. It then drains down another tube where it is fed back to the reservoir for re-circulation.

The NFT system provides nutrient solution to the roots without flooding them. The exposed root tops also receive oxygen, providing your plants with optimal conditions for fast and healthy growth. This system doesn't require the extensive setup and monitoring required by most other systems. As the water flows continuously, there's no need to worry about specific time schedules.

The only upkeep this system requires is a weekly change-out of the nutrient solution. Plus, you'll need little to no growing medium.

You can set this system up vertically or horizontally. The ideal arrangement will depend on the plants you wish to grow. It's also relatively easy to add additional channels to your system if you'd like to expand it. NFT systems are preferable for short-season crops like lettuce and herbs.

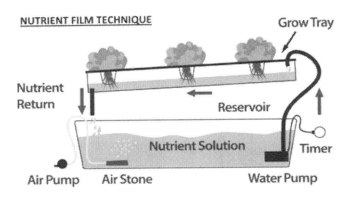

Illus. 25 – Nutrient Film Technique Set-Up

THE FIVE MAIN COMPONENTS OF AN NFT SYSTEM

- Reservoir
- Grow Tubes (also called Gullies or Channels)
- Growing Baskets, Medium, or Starter Cubes
- Submersible Pump
- Tubing

Reservoir

The size of your reservoir is dependent on the size of your system. Too small a reservoir will create instability in your nutrient solution.

- For small plants, supply a minimum of a ½ gallon of water per plant
- For medium plants, supply a minimum of 1 ½ gallons of water per plant
- For large plants, supply a minimum of 2 ½ gallons of water, per plant

The reservoir should be placed below the channels to ensure the pump operates effectively.

Grow Tubes (a.k.a. Channels or Gullies)

PVC, stainless steel, and rain guttering are common material choices for the channels. Wood channels can also work if they are lined with waterproof plastic. Avoid using heavy metals.

PVC is often used because it's inexpensive and easy to set up. The downside of PVC is its roundness, which can cause the nutrient-water to flow unevenly around the plant's roots. This is mainly a problem with larger plants. Flat channels will ensure effective water flow and prevent uneven root growth. There are also a number of hydroponic companies that make channels specifically for this system.

The width of your channel should be set to the size needed to accommodate the root systems of mature plants. Quick-growing plants like lettuce only need about four inches in width. Slightly larger plants like strawberries will need about six inches. Larger, longer-term plants such as tomatoes need approximately eight inches.

The channel should be covered to prevent sunlight from contacting the plant's roots. Removable covers are best because they will allow you to inspect the roots and check for blockages in the system.

Flow Rate and Channel Slope

When determining where to set up your channels and slope, take ceiling height into account and make sure there is adequate space for the plants to grow. The slope of the channel determines how fast the water will flow through the system. The recommended slope is a 1:30 or 1:40 ratio. This means that you will want a one inch drop for every 30 or 40 inches of horizontal length. The maximum channel length for this slope is 40 feet. If the slope is flatter, recommended channel length is 20 feet.

For small, quick-growing plants like herbs and lettuce, a flow rate of 5-1 liter per minute is recommended. For larger plants such as tomatoes, a flow rate of 2 liters per minute is recommended.

It's best to set your system up so that you can adjust the slope depending on your plants' needs. This will also allow you to clear the channel if roots grow to block the system.

The channels should be as straight as possible. Any sag or give in the material will cause water to pool and reduce the efficiency of the system.

Plants near the end of the channel will get less nutrients. For larger channels, you'll need to install a second reservoir to make sure all plants get enough nutrients.

Growing Baskets, Medium, or Starter Cubes

Net pots or other types of growing baskets can be set into the top or the cover of the channel. Holes must be cut for each basket. It's important to remember that the baskets should not touch the water. The roots need to dangle in the air with just the tips touching the water solution. If the roots need support while they are young, use clay pebbles as a growing medium to secure them. As the roots grow out, you will likely find that a growing medium becomes unnecessary.

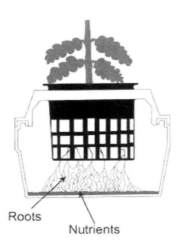

Illus. 26 – Net Pot, Roots And Nutrients

Starter cubes are excellent for this system and easy to use. You can start your seeds in the cube and transfer the entire cube into the NFT system when it's ready. Many NFT System growers use the starter cubes without a net pot or basket because the mass of roots is strong enough to support itself. Home and garden stores carry a wide variety of starter cubes.

Submersible Pump

Please see section on pumps for Ebb and Flow Systems.

Tubing

Please see the section on tubing for Ebb and Flow Systems.

HOW TO BUILD AN NFT HYDROPONIC SYSTEM WITH PVC PIPES

This design requires a drawn-out plan before you begin. The design will depend on where you want to place it and what you intend to grow. It can be hung from a ceiling, propped up on wooden stands, or placed on a table with a built-in slope. As this system is gravity-driven, the most important thing is the flow. One end of the channel must be higher than the other. But not too high! This particular design needs approximately 1" of a slope per 30-40" of horizontal length, depending on what you are growing.

Before you build this hydroponic system, decide where you will place it, what plants you will grow, and how you will give it the desired slope. Building the slope can be as simple as placing the system on a table and propping up one end with wedges. This system requires the use of a pump, so make sure your system is within reach of an electrical outlet.

What You Will Need:
- 4" PVC Pipe, 30" length
- 2 adjustable rubber end-caps for PVC with hose clamps
- Net pots or other grow containers
- Submersible pump
- Irrigation tubing (make sure it will fit the output of your pump)
- Plumbing cement
- Growing medium
- Plants
- Nutrients
- Reservoir container (20+ gallon size)
- Drill
- Hole Saw
- Tape measure
- Zip Ties, wire shelf hangers, assorted lumber to make a stand, or wooden wedges to make the necessary slope

Assembly:

1. Cut holes in the top of your PVC pipe for your net pots or growing containers. The number of holes you will need and their size will depend on what you're growing. Also, the distance between each plant/hole is important. If you would like 3" between each plant, measure 3" from one end of the PVC pipe. Cut out a circle that will fit your grow container. Measure another 3" and repeat until you get to the end of the PVC. [Make sure pots are NOT going to fall through the holes!]

2. Attach adjustable rubber caps to the ends of the PVC pipe.

3. Cut another hole in the top of the PVC to fit your tubing. This is where nutrient solution will be pumped in from the reservoir. Make sure the hole is the same size or a little smaller than your tubing so it fits snug.

4. On the opposite end of your PVC pipe cut a hole in the bottom to fit your tubing. This will drain the water to the reservoir. Make sure it is placed beyond where the roots will sit. You don't want it to drain before it reaches the last of your plants

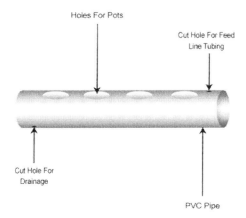

Illus. 27 – NFT System – PVC Pipe With Holes For Net Pots

5. Using the flow rate calculation discussed earlier, determine the ideal slope for your system.

6. You can use wire or zip ties to attach your PVC pipe to the ceiling of your room. Alternately, you can build a wooden stand with a slight incline, or place the system on a table and use wooden wedges to create the desired slope.

7. Cut two holes in the lid of the reservoir to fit your irrigation tubing. One is for output and the other for input.

8. Place the water pump in the bottom of the reservoir.

9. Attach the irrigation hose to the pump. Use plumbing cement if necessary to secure all seals. Feed the irrigation hose through one of the holes in your reservoir lid and lead it to the hole in your PVC pipe.

10. Connect another length of tubing from the hole in the bottom of the PVC pipe to the second hole in the lid of your reservoir. Use plumbing cement to secure the seal if necessary.

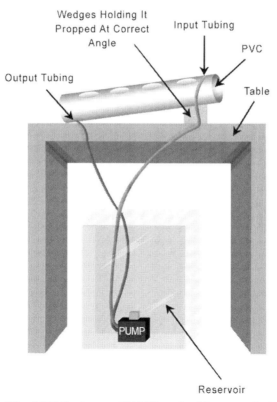

Illus. 28 – NFT System – PVC Pipe And Reservoir Set-Up

11. Fill your reservoir with water and nutrients as per package instructions.

12. Fill the growing containers with growing medium and plants and place them in the holes in the PVC.

13. Turn on your pump and test the system for leaks and slope/flow rate. Make sure the roots touch the flowing water.

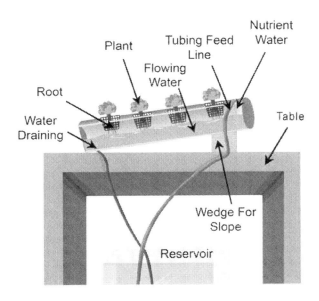

Illus. 29 – NFT System – Plant And Nutrient Water Set-Up

Caring For Your Plants In An NFT System:

- Check the pH often and adjust as needed.
- Inspect the pump regularly.
- Keep an eye on root growth. Make sure the roots don't block the channel.
- Inspect the tubing for blockages.
- Change out the nutrient solution weekly.

HOW TO SET UP AN AEROPONIC HYDROPONIC SYSTEM

The Aeroponic System is the most technical of the hydroponic systems. However, it's still easy for the home gardener to build. In an Aeroponic System, the plant's roots hang in mid-air in an enclosed system. They are regularly misted with nutrient solution. This way, the roots receive plenty of oxygen and other nutrients to maximize plant growth. Since the roots receive so much oxygen, the plants will grow more quickly with this system than with the others described above.

The main advantages of Aeroponic Systems are that they use minimal, if any, growing medium and less water than any other system.

The downside is that these systems are more expensive to build than others. Plus, the roots are susceptible to drying out since they are continuously exposed to the air. Any disruption in the irrigation system could destroy the entire crop. The sprinkler heads tend to clog so it is important to have spares on hand. It isn't a good idea to disrupt the water supply to the plants while cleaning the clogged heads. Instead, you can switch out the heads that are clogged so you can fix them without having to rush.

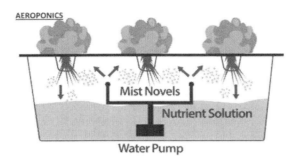

Illus. 30 – Aeroponics Set-Up

There are two types of Aeroponic system: Low-Pressure and High-Pressure. Most often when people talk about Aeroponic Systems, they're talking about the Low-Pressure variety. However, High-Pressure systems have distinct advantages. The main difference between the Low-Pressure and High-Pressure systems is the size of the water droplets. While this might seem like a small thing, it can mean a lot to your plants.

Low-Pressure Systems have larger water droplets. High-Pressure Systems, often called "true Aeroponics", employ very fine water droplets. With fine water droplets, the roots will be misted with nutrient solution. The plants receive more oxygen because they aren't being drenched by the nutrient solution. High-Pressure Systems are more complex and expensive to build than Low-Pressure Systems. However, if you can set one up, it will pay dividends in your plant growth.

Due to the relative ease in construction, this guide focuses primarily on Low-Pressure Hydroponics Systems.

THE SEVEN MAIN COMPONENTS OF AN AEROPONIC SYSTEM

- Enclosed Grow Chamber
- Net Pots (or other containers for plants)
- Misting/Sprinkler Heads
- Submersible Pump
- Reservoir
- Tubing
- Timer

Enclosed Grow Chamber

The grow chamber needs to be airtight and opaque so no light gets in. A large opaque tote bin will serve well for this purpose. Make sure it's tall enough for your roots to hang down without touching the bottom. Also, if your reservoir is directly below, make sure the roots won't touch the water.

Net Pots/Plant Containers

Please refer to the section on Net Pots for the Water Culture System.

Misting/Sprinkler Heads

The spray from your misting heads should overlap. When planning your design, keep this in mind. Make sure your setup ensures that all roots will be covered by the spray.

Misting heads are available from garden stores and online. There are many different types and sizes to choose from. It's best to look at reviews and read what other growers have used to find the best one for your situation. The ideal solution for you will depend on what you're growing and how you have designed the system.

Submersible Pump

Please refer to the section on pumps for Ebb and Flow Systems. With each added misting head, water pressure will drop. Keep this in mind when selecting a pump. This system needs a high HEAD rating.

Reservoir

Please see refer to the section on reservoirs for Ebb and Flow Systems. For the most simple setups, the reservoir and the grow chamber are the same size. However, different designs may require larger reservoirs.

Tubing

Please refer to the section on tubing for the Ebb and Flow System.

Timer

Please refer to the section on timers for the Ebb and Flow System.

HOW TO BUILD A 5-GALLON BUCKET LOW-PRESSURE AEROPONIC SYSTEM

This system can also be easily adapted for a large storage bin. Instead of one sprinkler though, there will be several connected with PVC pipe. You'll need a pump and timer, so place the bucket near an electrical outlet

What You Will Need:
- 1 5-gallon bucket with lid
- Net pots (the size will depend on what you are growing)
- Timer
- Pump
- 1 360-degree sprinkler head with 1/2" thread
- 1/2" x 12" threaded poly riser
- Hole saw
- Drill
- Regular saw

Assembly:

1. Cut holes in the lid of the bucket to fit your net pots. Space them out evenly. Make sure pots will not fall all the way through but will fit snugly.

2. Screw the threaded poly riser into the pump. Cut it to the desired height.

3. Attach the sprinkler head to the top of the poly riser. The height of both riser and sprinkler head should be lower than the expected length of the roots.

4. Place the pump with attached riser and sprinkler head onto the bottom of the bucket.

5. Lead the cord for the pump out through one of the holes in the lid and attach it to the timer.

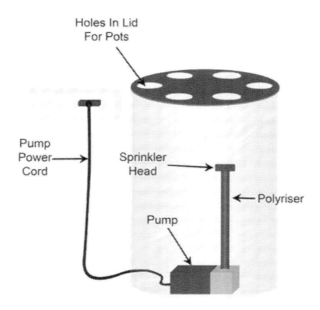

Illus. 31 – 5-Gallon Bucket Aeroponic Set-Up

6. Fill the bucket with 2 gallons of water and the appropriate amount of nutrients as per package directions.

7. Secure the lid on top of the bucket. Arrange the plants in the net pots. Clay pebbles can be used to keep them in place if necessary.

8. Turn the pump on.

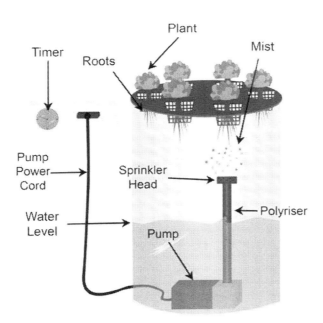

Illus. 32 – 5-Gallon Bucket Aeroponics – Plants And Nutrient Water Set-Up

Caring For Your Plants in An Aeroponic System:

• Pay close attention to the temperature in your grow space. It's all too easy to cook the exposed roots of your plants. Grow lights can exacerbate the problem if you're not careful. It may be necessary to invest in an air conditioner or use more efficient lights. Between spray cycles, the roots will be exposed and fragile. Treat them carefully!

• The reservoir temperature should be kept at 64F or slightly below. If the water is too hot, it will burn the roots.

• Clean filters, pumps, and tubing regularly. The biggest rookie mistake is to allow clogged nozzles to go unnoticed. This can endanger plant growth, from one plant to the entire crop. Thankfully, this is completely preventable if you keep a close eye on the system and keep fresh nozzles to hand.

• In this system, everything happens faster. The plants grow quicker, which is great. The other side of this, though, is that problems will develop faster and impact the plants more quickly. Be diligent.

This concludes the building guide for all six hydroponic systems. I know there's a lot to think about. However, one of the great things about hydroponic systems is their adaptability. Try out a few of these systems and see which one works best for you.

In the following chapters, we'll explore the pro tips for making your system the most successful it can be and achieving maximum healthy plant growth.

CHAPTER 4: GROWING MEDIUMS, NUTRIENTS & LIGHTING

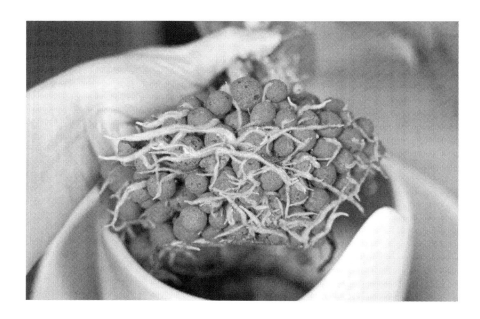

In nature, plants rely upon soil for stability and nutrients. Since hydroponic systems use no soil, the plants need to be stabilized and obtain nutrients in other ways. This chapter will help you determine which growing medium is best for your system. We'll also address different nutrient choices and lighting methods. Mediums, nutrients, and lighting are vitally important for the health of your plants.

With regard to medium, growers have plenty of options. Many people end up using a mix of different mediums. The ideal mix depends on availability in your area. Nutrients are produced by several different commercial companies, and each has pros and cons. Once you understand how to interpret the numbers on the bottle, you'll be much better prepared to decide which is best for your system. Lighting is pretty straight-forward. If your system has access to the sun, then you won't need to consider lighting at all. On the other hand, appropriate lighting is a necessity for indoor growing.

GROWING MEDIUMS

As mentioned before, you have many choices when it comes to growing mediums. The ideal medium for your system depends on which hydroponic system you are using and what you are growing. Common growing mediums are rockwool, coco coir, peat moss, clay pellets, perlite, vermiculite, and gravel.

ROCKWOOL

Rockwool comes in slabs, blocks, and loose fill. It is an inorganic substance, made by melting rocks and spinning them into long, fine fibers. In this sense, it is similar to fiberglass.

Rockwool blocks are great for starting seedlings. In many

systems, you don't even have to remove the seedlings from the Rockwool to add them to your system. Simply transfer the entire block with plant to your grow pot.

Rockwool naturally has a high pH level. Because of this, it is necessary to soak it before use. It's also difficult to dispose of properly as the thin fibers won't biodegrade. In essence, they'll last forever.

The high-absorbency of Rockwool makes it a great choice for the Drip System. However, it can become over-saturated so you'll need to monitor the system carefully.

COCO COIR

Coco coir is made of ground coconut husks. It is quickly becoming a popular choice amongst hydroponic growers. In nature, coconut husks protect coconuts from sun, sea, and salt damage. When the coconut is ready to sprout, the husk will act as a natural growing medium. By using ground coconut husks in your hydroponic garden, you'll provide these same advantages for your own plants. Coco coir is a renewable, sustainable material. It also looks very much like soil, making it appealing to those who prefer a more natural approach.

Coco coir can hold up to ten times its weight in water. This is great for a hydroponic system. At the same time, it can cause your system to retain too much water. Because of this, Coco Coir is not recommended for constant-flow systems.

Coco coir comes in compressed dry bricks that need to be

rehydrated before use. This adds a little extra work to the hydroponic process, but it's not difficult and won't take much time.

If you use coco coir, it's important to choose a nutrient mix specifically designed for this medium. Coco coir binds with iron and magnesium and can starve your plants of these essential elements.

This medium works wonderfully when mixed 50/50 with perlite. Coco Coir retains nutrient solution, while perlite retains oxygen.

EXPANDED CLAY PELLETS

Also referred to as Hydroton, clay pellets are great for many reasons. The clay pellets expand in water to make round, porous balls. Their round shape is stable enough to hold a seedling in place without denying it oxygen or water. These elements can still flow freely around the plant's roots.

One thing to consider is that clay pellets are heavy compared to most mediums. If you fill an entire grow tray with them, you may have a weight issue. Plus, the pellets can dry out quickly because there is so much space between them. If you're not careful, this can cause your roots to dry out, stopping plant growth altogether.

Clay pellets are great for a Drip System because you can run the dripper constantly without worrying about over-saturation or excess dryness.

PERLITE

Perlite is aerated volcanic rock. It is light and porous and has been used for years in both soil and hydroponic gardens. Perlite is excellent for retaining oxygen levels. The downside is that it is light in weight. It can easily get washed away or shifted from where you want it. For this reason, it is commonly mixed with another medium, like coco coir or vermiculite.

VERMICULITE

Vermiculite is a mineral that expands when heated and forms a pebble shape. It holds water and wicks well, meaning it will draw water and nutrients upwards. The downsides are that it can hold too much water and it is more expensive than most other mediums. If you choose to include vermiculite in your mix, the best option is to blend a small amount of it with other mediums.

GRAVEL

Gravel is the cheapest material you can use. If you're on a tight budget, this is the material for you. You'll need to wash it before you use it, to protect the sensitive roots of your plants from any harmful bacteria or other detrimental substances that may be present. Another downside is that it's quite heavy. If you use lots of gravel, you'll need to make sure your system has enough structural stability to handle it.

STARTER PLUGS/CUBES

Starter plugs are small, compact masses of material used to start seedlings. There is a hole in the top of the plug for the seed to be placed. Once they are watered, seeds will germinate in starter plugs faster than in soil or other materials. They contain all the nutrients that your seeds need to get started. Some starter plugs even come with seeds already in them.

Starter plugs can be made of a number of different materials. The most common materials are Rockwool, peat moss, and pine pulp. If they dry out, it can be hard to rehydrate them, so make sure to keep them sufficiently watered.

The biggest benefit of starter plugs in a hydroponic system is that the seedlings don't need to be transplanted. They can be placed directly into your system without being removed from the plug.

Types of Mediums

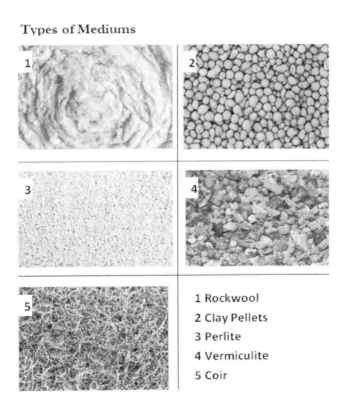

1 Rockwool
2 Clay Pellets
3 Perlite
4 Vermiculite
5 Coir

Growing Medium Notes

Please note that I do not include peat moss in this list. Even though it has been commonly used in hydroponic systems, it is not a renewable resource. If you'd like to learn more about this, do a little digging. There's plenty of available information which explains in-depth the environmental impact of extensive peat moss use.

NUTRIENTS

Since hydroponic systems don't use soil, the nutrients added to the water must contain all the minerals plants need to thrive. The selection of the appropriate nutrient solution is one of the most important decisions of your hydroponic plan. Healthy plant growth depends on having the right balance of nutrients.

There are 16 essential elements that plants need. These elements are absorbed by the plant in different ways. Some are transferred to the plant through the roots, while others are taken in through the pores of the leaf. Carbon, Oxygen, and Hydrogen, three of the most necessary elements, can be obtained from both air and water. These need to be monitored and balanced. One common problem in hydroponics is a lack of sufficient carbon dioxide.

The next big three elements, Nitrogen, Phosphorus, and Potassium, are provided in the fertilizer nutrient blends made for growing hydroponic plants. A fine balance of these is extremely important. This is often referred to as the N-P-K mix. When looking at bottles or bags of fertilizer, you'll see a list of three numbers on the front, separated by dashes. It will look something like this: 3-4-1. These three numbers refer to the Nitrogen, Phosphorus, and Potassium (N-P-K) proportion of the mix.

Calcium, Magnesium, and Sulfur are the next most essential elements. They are also supplied by fertilizer supplements. Calcium is provided through a calcium nitrate ($CaNO_3$) fertilizer. Magnesium and Sulfur are available with magnesium sulfate (MgSO4) supplements.

The remaining 7 essential elements, Copper, Zinc, Boron, Molybdenum, Iron, Manganese, and Chlorine, are rarely deficient. If there is an Iron deficiency, you can supplement your plants with chelated iron. The remaining 7 essential elements, Copper, Zinc, Boron, Molybdenum, Iron, Manganese, and Chlorine, are rarely deficient. If there is an Iron deficiency, you can supplement your plants with chelated iron.

To make sure your plants get everything they need, specially crafted fertilizer mixes are made for hydroponic crops. These mixes can be added to the water in your reservoir and distributed to your plants through the hydroponic system. Specific fertilizers are created for specific crops. They're not all interchangeable. The hydroponic nutrient mix for tomatoes will be quite different from the one for lettuce.

Nutrient mixes are available as liquid or granules. Liquid fertilizer is easy to use. You just pour it into the water reservoir as per the bottle's instructions. The downside to using liquid fertilizer is that it is more expensive and bulkier to store. Granulated fertilizer is more cost effective, easier to store, and often comes in bulk. However, it isn't as easy to use because it has to be mixed prior to use and it doesn't always dissolve completely. Either one will work fine, so it's a matter of personal preference and what's required by your particular system.

Granulated mixes are available in three types. The one-part

mixes are simple and straight-forward. The fertilizer is mixed as indicated on the bag. These are simple to use, but not the best for making stock solutions. Some nutrients in high concentration will form solids. A multi-part solution is better for making stock solutions because the compounds are kept separately. They are relatively easy to mix, too. This is the most common choice for growers who are using granulated nutrient mixes. However, the multi-part mixes can be expensive, so it isn't the best choice unless you have a very large garden operation.

Hydroponic fertilizer mixes are also specialized for different stages of growth. They will indicate on the package the stage of growth for which they are designed. Examples of growth stages include vegetative (leaf growth) or blooming (flowering). You'll want to know what you actually want from the plant. Spinach, lettuce, and kale, for example, will benefit most from vegetative growth because you harvest the leaves of the plant. For plants that deliver a fruit or flower, you'll want to use the vegetative mix up to the point where you want them to flower. Then, switch to the flowering mix.

Nutrients are further classified based on the growing medium that is being used. The majority of nutrient mixes are made for a specific growing medium. Pay attention to package specifics and do your homework. If you're using a vermiculite mix but your growth medium is clay pellets, then you won't get optimal results. If the package doesn't give you all the details you need, then a simple online search will lead you in the right direction.

Hydroponic nutrients can be organic or synthetic. Organic

fertilizers are best for systems that recirculate or reuse the nutrient solution. These mixes often include materials that can clog up sprayers, drip lines, and pumps. Synthetic nutrients don't have this issue and are therefore more commonly used in hydroponic systems. Organic fertilizers will often have a lower N-P-K listing than synthetic. However, this doesn't mean they are of a lower quality. Synthetic mixes are generally fast-release, as opposed to the slow-release of organic, and so the readily available N-P-K is higher in the synthetic. However, organic mixes will deliver a natural, time release fertilizer that won't burn your roots.

NUTRIENTS YOU NEED FOR YOUR HYDROPONIC SYSTEM

- An N-P-K mix, formulated for the crop you are growing
- Calcium Nitrate (CaNO3)
- Magnesium Sulfate (MgSO4)

HOW TO ADD NUTRIENTS TO YOUR HYDROPONIC SYSTEM

1. Mix the solution as per the package instructions and add it to your reservoir.

2. Check your pH balance on a daily or weekly basis. (This timing will depend on the system you are using and the crops you are growing.)

3. Change out or top off your solution weekly or bi-weekly. (Again, the timing depends on the system and crops).

4. Flush your crop before harvesting. (Flushing your hydroponic crop means allowing it to grow without nutrient solution for a brief period prior to harvesting.)

TESTING THE PH

pH is the balance of acidity and alkalinity of your water. The nutrients you add to your water will influence the acid/alkaline balance. pH is measured on a scale from 0-14, with 0 being the most acidic and 14 being the most alkaline or basic. pH tests will tell you how well the plants will be able to use the nutrients. Each plant prefers a specific pH balance, and your plants won't be able to absorb the needed nutrients if the pH is too high or too low. Measure the pH after you've added the nutrients and then adjust as needed. A good baseline is to keep it between 5.5 and 6.5.

pH testing devices include paper litmus test strips, liquid test kits, and electronic testing pens. Paper test strips are the cheapest way to go, but they lack accuracy. Litmus strips change color when you dip them in solution. The resultant color reflects the pH. But checking the resulting color against the chart is a bit subjective, so you won't be able to determine the acidity of the solution with any amount of precision. The results can also be skewed if your nutrient solution isn't clear, which is a problem because many nutrient solutions will color the water.

Liquid test kits offer a fair balance of cost and precision. To use a liquid test kit, you take a small sample of solution and place it into a vial which contains a pH-sensitive dye. As with the litmus test, you will compare the resulting color with a chart. This will help you to determine the pH balance of your solution. The color changes are easier to see, and the test is a bit more sensitive than a litmus test, so the liquid test kit is somewhat more accurate. However, liquid test kits can also be skewed by the color of your solution (if it's not clear), so they aren't 100% accurate. However, unless your plants are extremely sensitive, liquid test kits are accurate enough.

If your number one consideration is accuracy in pH testing, digital meters are the way to go. They are more expensive, but they will tell you the pH to a tenth, and they won't be skewed by the color of your nutrient solution. To use a digital meter, you just insert the tip of the meter in the solution and it will provide you with a digital reading. The one thing you have to watch out for with these meters is calibration. To calibrate them, you must dip them in a pH neutral solution to provide a baseline. This is easier than it sounds, and you can find plenty of information about it online if you need.

If you need to adjust the pH, phosphoric acid will raise acidity (lower pH) and lemon juice will lower acidity (raise pH). There are also a number of pH adjustment products readily available in hydroponic stores.

FLUSHING

The nutrients you feed your plants build up in them and can cause bitter or chemical tastes. Flushing out the plants before harvesting ensures a good end product. Do this for 4-7 days prior to the harvest. The most traditional way to do this is to irrigate your plants with pure water and allow them to process it through their system for up to a week before harvesting. If you'd like to get fancy, several flushing agents are readily available at hydroponic stores. They'll speed up the process and ensure a complete flush. Remember – flushing is extremely important. You'll be able to taste the difference, regardless of what it is you're growing.

OPTIONAL ADDITIVES FOR THE PLANTS
Bloom Maximizers

These are added to your nutrient solution to increase the size and yield of your plants. They are usually high in Phosphorus and Potassium. This additive can be quite expensive, but it's generally worth the price for the boost it gives the plants. Nutrient burn can be a problem when using this so monitor the plants closely if you choose to use it. (Nutrient burn is the plant's equivalent of chemical burn. If you see the roots turn a different color, take on an unhealthy texture, or shrivel after adding the solution, flush the reservoir with pure water so that the plants can recover. It's far better, though, to make sure that you use the right concentration and you don't have to resort to damage control.) Bloom maximizers should only be used during the flowering stage of growth.

Mycorrhizae and Other Fungi

Mycorrhizae are small fungal filaments that penetrate the roots, increasing their surface area. They also gather and break down certain nutrients. Mycorrhizae exist in a symbiotic relationship with nearly all plant species. They help plants to absorb nutrients and water. In return, they receive some of the sugars that plants create through photosynthesis.

Mycorrhizal fungi can be added directly to the nutrient solution and will grow alongside the roots as they do in nature. You can also add other fungi such as Trichoderma to aid in breaking down nutrients and making your crops more resistant to soil pests. Trichoderma and Mycorrhizal fungi are readily available in hydroponics stores. They will help your plants to remain healthy and grow more quickly.

Vitamins and Enzymes

Thiamine (vitamin B-1) supports and strengthens the immune system of plants so they can better withstand stress and disease. It also facilitates root development, making the plants more resistant to shock and helping them to take in nutrients more quickly. This is especially important when transplanting. Enzymes break down nutrients, making them easier for plants to absorb. They are also helpful for preventing algae growth.

Root Stimulators

Root stimulators are compounds that replicate the benefits of natural soil. There are beneficial microbes in soil that promote plant growth, just as there are harmful microbes that interfere with plant growth. Rooting stimulators introduce the healthy microbes into your hydroponics system, helping your plants to have stronger immune systems, more access to nitrogen, and faster root development. They are also excellent at preventing bacterial complications in the root structure.

Overall, root stimulators promote fast, healthy plant growth. If you add root stimulators at the beginning of your growing cycle, they will continue to reproduce throughout your plants growth from seedling to harvest, providing more robust, faster-growing crops from the start.

Nutrient Notes:

When searching for nutrients, you will encounter a slew of brands and products. While they'll all claim to be the best, there's a great deal of variety in quality from one brand to the next, even among products designed for the same purpose. A brand or company might be good for one thing, but not so great for another.

The best way to deal with this is to read reviews from several growers to find out which products they prefer. This will provide you with solid feedback from people who have been there. Find hydroponic forums where you can post the details of your system and crop. You'll get plenty of responses from experienced growers that will direct you to products that have worked for them in similar situations.

Water quality is of utmost importance in a hydroponic system. Do not underestimate the necessity of good clean water. Distilled or RO (reverse osmosis) water is the best choice. Tap water or city water can have pollutants, chemicals, additives, and any number of things that can potentially have a negative impact on plant growth. This being said, plants use lots of water. If your prime concern is economy, then you'll use what you've got. Just remember that you get out of the plant what you put into it.

LIGHTING

Plants needs around twelve hours of light per day. Of course, this will vary depending on the plant that you are growing. Some plants prefer a great deal of light, while others do quite well with only a moderate amount. Remember that plants get their energy from light. If your hydroponic system isn't in a place where it is getting natural light from the sun, you'll need to set up a lighting system.

Plants have rhythms, just like we do. Look into the preferred light cycles of your plants, and set up timers so that you give them a schedule as close as possible to their natural cycle. The optimal light schedule will differ depending on the growth stage of the plant as well. Many plants grow well vegetatively when provided with constant light, but need cycles of light and darkness to trigger flowering.

The type of lighting you need depends on a wide variety of factors specific to your system: enclosure type, plant type, system size, ventilation, and last but not least, budget. Fluorescent tubes are good for a single low-budget system. Small systems will fare better with CFLs (Compact Fluorescent Lamps). These lights were designed as an efficient alternative to incandescent bulbs. They screw into a standard socket and provide sufficient light, but you may want to arrange reflectors so that the light is focused on the plant.

HIDs (High Intensity Discharge lamps) are another option. They are a bit more costly than CFLs, but they are a preferred lighting option for experienced growers. This is because they have a very high light output and are four to eight times more efficient than standard incandescent bulbs. However, they produce a lot of heat, so you'll have to ventilate your system to prevent it from drying out.

Another option is to use LEDs (Light Emitting Diode lamps). This is the high-tech option and will cost quite a bit more at the beginning, but they use a fraction of the electricity of other options and produce less heat. LEDs can also be calibrated to produce the exact spectrum of light that your plant needs. If you only plan to grow one crop, it's probably not worth it to purchase LEDs. But, if this is the beginning of a long relationship with hydroponic growing, they will more than pay off in the long run.

FLUORESCENT LIGHTS

Fluorescent lights are available in a wide range of sizes and spectrums. They are not ideal for large plants but they will work. They are generally inexpensive, easy to set up, and will work in a pinch.

COMPACT FLUORESCENT BULBS

These are a good choice because they aren't too expensive and they don't require any special wiring or set-up (they screw into a regular light socket). They produce light in all directions and are best used with a reflector so you don't waste any heat or light.

HIGH-INTENSITY DISCHARGE (HID) LIGHTS

HID lights have a high light output and are a preferred choice for growers. Using HIDs will be better for your plants than fluorescents and less expensive than incandescent bulbs in the long run. At the same time, they are expensive, require a special set-up, and need ventilation because of their high heat output.

LED LIGHTS

LED lights can provide the exact spectrum of light your plant needs. They last longer than all other lights and use less electricity. The upfront cost, however, is imposing. As mentioned above, LEDs are worth it if you plant to be growing many crops over the years. For a one-off, though, you may be better off with a different option.

CHAPTER 5: HOW TO MAINTAIN A HYDROPONIC SYSTEM

As with any garden venture, your hydroponic system will require maintenance to keep your plants healthy and your system operating well. You won't have to weed plants beds or mess with soil. Instead, you'll have to keep a close eye on a number of factors: temperature, water level, nutrient level, and cleanliness. Maintaining each of these factors is vital to the healthy growth of your crop. Monitor your system on a regular basis to make sure everything is working properly.

CLEANLINESS

Clean the grow space before you set up your system. Clean your grow boxes, reservoirs, grow pots and any other equipment you are using. This is best done with a 10% bleach solution.

Any leaves, flowers, or organic matter that falls off your plants should be cleared away immediately. Don't leave it lying around. This will encourage pests and diseases to take hold, as they thrive on dead plant matter.

NUTRIENT SOLUTION

It is recommended that you completely change out the nutrient water solution in your reservoir weekly. In some cases, it's okay to just top up the water. However, if you have an imbalance of micronutrients or a disease is trying to take hold, a top-up won't prevent it.

WATERING

"How much water do I need to use?" This is the most common question asked by new hydroponic growers and the most difficult to answer. The answer is completely dependent on what kind of system you have, what plants you are growing, the growing medium, surrounding temperature, etc. Here's the rule of thumb: Water enough to keep the roots wet, but not so much that they remain saturated.

If you notice the growing medium and roots getting dry between watering cycles, increase the irrigation frequency. If they seem to be wet all the time, decrease the frequency. The frequency can be adjusted as many times as you need until you have it correct for your system. Remember that as your plants grow, their water needs will change.

In general, there is no need to water at night. Plants absorb the most water when it is light outside. They don't use much during the dark hours. When you set up your timer, plan the irrigation cycles for the daylight hours. If you notice that your plants are getting dry at night, add a nighttime watering cycle as well.

RESERVOIR TEMPERATURE

The temperature of the water in your reservoir should be around 70F. If you struggle to maintain this temperature, consider getting a heating mat and placing it below the reservoir. Alternately, you can put a heating element inside the reservoir. If you have a small reservoir, an aquarium heater will work well.

If the temperature is too hot, try adding clean ice packs to the reservoir. Wrapping the reservoir in foil to deflect heat is another option that is both easy and inexpensive. If these methods don't work, you can purchase a water chiller. This is a coiled element that cools water. It can be installed in the reservoir to keep the temperature down.

HUMIDITY

Humidity and temperature are not the same thing. They serve separate purposes and both need to be monitored closely. Your plant's needs will change over time. Keep this in mind when checking temperature and humidity levels. Different types of plants also have different needs.

During the initial growth stage of a seedling the humidity needs to be above 80%. This is only for when the seeds are germinating. After this, the humidity should be lowered to promote plant growth.

For most plants, ideal humidity is between 50% and 65%. It must be at least 45%. Humidity can be hard to control. However, as you read in the pests and diseases section, it is extremely important. Too much humidity can be devastating for your plants. Too little can cause your plant to dry out. One of the best pieces of advice regarding humidity is to get a hygrometer for your grow space!

Seasonal temperatures where you live can affect the humidity of your grow space, even if it is indoors. The ventilation in your space will also have a huge impact on the humidity. Check humidity on a regular basis to account for natural fluctuations.

If you need to add humidity, get a vaporizer or humidifier. Another option, although not a great one, is to use a spray bottle and spray water around the room. It isn't a very good option because it will get all your equipment wet as well. If you need to decrease the humidity, the best option is to increase ventilation. Increased air flow will sweep away excess moisture in the air. A simple fan (or two or three) will work wonders. Dehumidifiers or air conditioners also do an excellent job of reducing humidity.

Humidity is also affected by the number of plants being grown and how densely they are arranged. Many plants close to one another will create a windbreak that doesn't allow fresh air to flow through. If the plants are spaced too closely together, the water vapor they exude will have nowhere to go.

If you'd like to get a little fancier, you can hook up a hygrometer to a fan and have it run automatically when it senses increased humidity.

INSPECT THE EQUIPMENT

Pumps, timers, aerators, tubing, and connectors can all fail. Plus, it can take hours or days before your plants begin to show the effects caused by malfunctioning equipment. Checking your equipment regularly will prevent situations before they reach challenging proportions.

LOOK AT YOUR PLANTS!

Really look at them. Look under the leaves, examine the roots, take notice of any abnormalities on a day-to-day basis. Monitor growth patterns. If you are keeping a close eye on them, you will notice when things look off or when something has gone wrong.

Check the water levels regularly and test the nutrient levels and pH regularly. Every 3-4 days at a minimum. Every day is better.

TAKE NOTES!

Check on your plants. Take note of how much nutrient solution they are using, how big they are growing, which nutrients you are using, and how much water they are getting if they're on a timer. You won't regret this, I promise. After you have completed one grow cycle, it helps 100-fold with your next cycle to have detailed notes of what worked and what didn't, as well as any problems that were encountered and how they were overcome.

CHANGE ONE THING AT A TIME

When you are making adjustments to your system, change only one thing at a time. If you change multiple things, it becomes hard to know exactly what fixed the problem. And, if your changes cause another problem, it will be difficult to ascertain exactly why. Make changes in increments. Record the results each time.

CHAPTER 6: POTENTIAL PROBLEMS AND HOW TO OVERCOME THEM

While we'd all like to hope that our plants and systems won't encounter any of these issues, it's good to know the signs so you can easily identify them if they do occur. A lot of the pests and diseases you may encounter in hydroponic gardening are the same as those you would encounter with soil gardening. Since the hydroponic system is relatively closed and protected, your chances of encountering these problems are less than if you were gardening in soil. However, there are other problems which are unique to a hydroponic system. As with any type of gardening, diligence will go a long way towards keeping your system strong and your plants healthy.

PESTS

The potential for pests in a hydroponic system is lower than in a soil-based system. This doesn't mean that it is impossible to get them though. The main issue with pests is that because the system is so interconnected, if the problem goes unnoticed or unattended to, the end result can be devastating. Make sure you understand the telltale signs for each type of pest so that if you do see something unusual, you can act on it immediately.

THRIPS

Thrips are tough to see because they are so small. However, the damage they cause is hard to miss. If your plants are infested with thrips, tiny metallic black spots will appear on the tips of the leaves. Following this, the leaves will turn yellow, then they will turn brown and dry out. Thrips are parasitic insects that leech the life from your plants, preventing them from nourishing leaf growth.

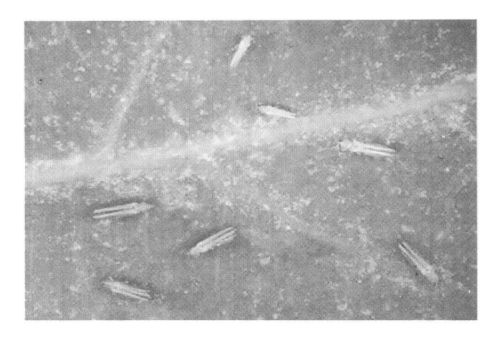

APHIDS

Commonly referred to as plant lice, aphids suck the juice of leaves, turning them yellow. Aphids can be green, black, or gray. They are usually found gathered around plant stems.

SPIDER MITES

Unfortunately, these common pests are almost impossible to notice until you see the damage to your plants as they are so tiny. To determine if you have a spider mite infestation, check for spider-like webbing around the leaves and stem. Also, gently wipe the underside of the leaves with a tissue and check for spider mite blood.

FUNGUS GNATS

The larvae of this pest are what cause the damage. Adult gnats are not harmful to your plant at all. However, the larvae feed on roots and can stunt growth, cause infections, and ultimately kill the plant.

WHITE FLIES

These are relatively easy to spot because they look like very small white moths. The problem is that they fly away when disturbed and are hard to catch. They will cause white spots and yellowing of your plants.

HOW TO COMBAT PESTS

• Place sticky traps around the room and at the base of your plants. Yellow sticky traps are good for catching fungus gnats and white flies. Blue sticky traps attract thrips.

• Pesticides and sprays are good options as long as they are not poisonous or potentially harmful to you or your plants. Look for organic options.

- Beneficial predators such as nematodes, can be placed into your growing medium so they can hunt and kill any pests.

- Inspect your plants regularly! Don't neglect the base of the stem or underneath the leaves.

DISEASES

In general, the probability of diseases in hydroponics is less because there is no soil to encourage or start them. Fungus and bacteria thrive in soil. The most common cause of disease in a hydroponic system is environmental conditions. While this requires constant monitoring, it also means that it can be controlled. Diseases are likely to spread in crowded conditions, so make sure the plants have enough space to grow individually and that you can take out infected plants if necessary.

You can also protect your plants from disease by introducing root stimulators to your system during the early growth stages. These are the equivalent of probiotics for your plants. Trichoderma, enzymes, and thiamine can also be helpful in combating harmful pathogens and keeping your plants' immune systems strong.

Your plants will be better able to resist pathogens if they are supplied with enough nutrients (not too little and not too much) and the pH level of the system is kept within healthy parameters. Imbalances will weaken the plants' immune system, making them susceptible to opportunistic pathogens.

As with pest issues, it is best to avoid the use of any harsh chemicals. They can get into your nutrient solution, accumulate in the leaves and stems of your plants, and cause poisoning. If you must use strong chemicals, cover your water supply and spray as sparingly as possible.

ROOT ROT

This disease causes your plants to wilt and turn yellow. The roots will often turn mushy as well. It is caused by too much water and/or pathogens in your growing medium. To avoid root rot, keep the moisture levels balanced and follow the advice above regarding diseases.

GRAY MOLD

This starts out as small spots on the plant's leaves. Soon, the leaves will turn gray and fuzzy and continue to deteriorate until the plant is mushy and brown. It is often called ash mold or ghost spot. It is caused by a fungus and is more common in humid areas.

POWDERY MILDEW

If it looks like someone sprinkled baby powder all over your plants, then you most likely have powdery mildew. This disease is a fungal infection. It will stunt plant growth, yellow the leaves, and eventually cause the leaves to drop. If left untreated, it can kill your plant. Too much humidity will encourage powdery mildew.

DOWNY MILDEW

Similar to powdery mildew, except it doesn't look like powder, downy mildew leaves white markings on your plant and causes yellowing of leaves. It occurs in overly wet weather, or when leaves are wet for too long. Downy mildew is usually found on the underside of leaves.

IRON DEFICIENCY

Iron deficiency causes the veins of the leaves to remain green while the remainder of the leaf turns bright yellow. The solution is fairly simple though. Introduce chelated iron to your nutrient solution and your plants will begin to look healthier in no time. You'll be able to find chelated iron at your local hydroponics store.

CALCIUM DEFICIENCY

If your plants are experiencing calcium deficiency, the young leaves on the plant will curl downwards. This is caused by a lack of water movement within the plant. Calcium is not in the nutrient mix; it comes from supplements or from the water itself. Humidity levels have a high impact on the amount of calcium a plant can absorb. High humidity reduces the amount of calcium a plant can take in.

RUST

Small red bumps will appear on the undersides of the leaves. The leaves will then turn yellow, then brown, and then die. This disease is caused by high humidity and is extremely contagious. Unfortunately, only harsh chemicals will treat this.

HOW TO COMBAT DISEASES

1. The best combat for any disease is prevention. Monitor closely and act quickly. Excessive humidity is the most common cause of the disease. Monitor the humidity of your grow space by buying a hygrometer. These are inexpensive and entirely worth it.

2. Keep air circulating with an air conditioner or fan so it doesn't become stale and encourage disease growth.

3. Do not over water your plants!

4. Remove any infected leaves and discard them outside or away from your grow space.

SYSTEM PROBLEMS

Hydroponic systems, whether homemade or store bought, suffer from a few common problems apart from pests and diseases. These challenges include algae bloom, nutrient deficiency, and system clogging.

ALGAE BLOOM

Algae are small aquatic plant organisms. They appear on the

surface of the nutrient-enriched water and can look like a stain or a slimy film. Not all algae are green; they can vary widely in color. Algae can be green, black, red, or brown. It can smell like mold or dirt, especially as it decomposes. The problem with algae is that it consumes nutrients and oxygen in the reservoir and blocks irrigation lines, hoses, and pumps. Algae also attracts fungus gnats which like to eat the roots of your plants.

As algae are plants, they thrive under the same conditions that nurture all plants: light, nutrients, warmth, and moisture. Nutrients, warmth, and moisture can't be adjusted much in the reservoir; these are necessary and need to be maintained within parameters for optimal plant growth. Light, on the other-hand, can be controlled. Light shining into or onto the reservoir can be reduced or blocked out almost entirely.

The simplest solution is to negate the issue from the beginning. Use a reservoir that is dark colored or spray paint a clear one with a dark color. Another option is to create a light shield that fits around the reservoir. This can be made simply with cardboard, cut to fit around the sides. A removable protective sleeve is preferred so you can still see into the reservoir if needed.

Algae can also bloom on top of your growing medium, especially if you are using a top-watering method such as the Drip System. Here, you can't block the light from hitting the water solution since it is at the base of your plants.

The best way to deal with any algae growth is to clean everything. If you have algae in the reservoir, the next time you are changing out the nutrient solution, dump everything out and scrub all surfaces with a sterilizing solution. If algae appears on the growing medium, wash it thoroughly with clean water. This may be difficult if the plant is entrenched in the medium. You may have to wait until after the plants are harvested to give everything a thorough scrubbing.

Be careful of using any commercial sterilizing solutions or agents in the reservoir while the plants are growing. Since algae is a plant, anything that kills it could potentially kill your plants.

NUTRIENT DEFICIENCY

Nutrients and the lack thereof can have a massive impact on your hydroponic system. Plants depend upon nutrients for healthy growth. Nutrient deficiency often occurs if the plants use the solution more quickly than it is replaced. If you see signs of nutrient deficiency, reevaluate how often you are changing the nutrient solution or adding nutrients. You may need to replenish them more often.

If adjusting the frequency of nutrient solution doesn't fix the problem, there are some other options. To reverse nutrient deficiency, supplement the enriched water with the missing nutrient. If that doesn't work, you may need to change the type or brand of nutrient solution you are using.

It can be difficult to identify a nutrient deficiency and the specific nutrient which needs to be supplemented. A deficiency of one element can lead to a deficiency in another, leading to a cascade effect and confusing symptoms. Often, any deficiency is an indication of a larger problem with your system. Try to look for the source of the problem as well as treating the symptom.

Below is a list of the vital nutrients and the signs of specific deficiencies:

Nitrogen: stunted plant growth, lower leaves are yellow, entire plant is light green

Phosphorous: plant is blue-green in color, stunted growth, dries to greenish brown and then black (don't forget, some plants naturally have blue or green leaves!)

Potassium: dead spots on leaf edges, leaves are papery in appearance, stunted growth

Magnesium: lower leaves are wilted and yellow around the edges

Calcium: new plant growth, leaves and stems die

Zinc: the spaces between the veins of the leaves are yellowish and have a papery appearance

Iron: veins remain strong green while the remainder of the leaf is yellow

Copper: edges of leaves curl up and look blue or dark green

Sulfur: stunted, spindly growth, older leaves remain green while new ones turn yellowy green

Manganese: stunted growth, bottom leaves are checkered yellow and green

Molybdenum: stunted, malformed, yellow leaves

Boron: scorched tips on new leaves

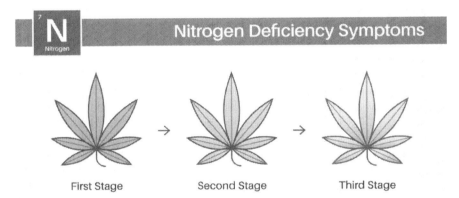

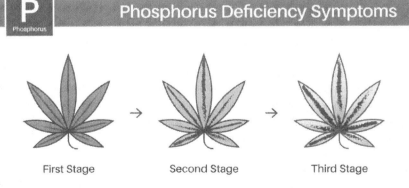

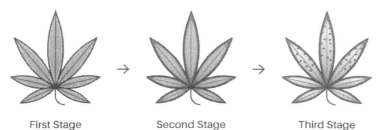

First Stage	Second Stage	Third Stage

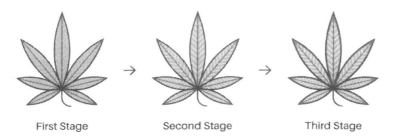

First Stage	Second Stage	Third Stage

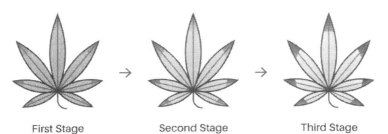

First Stage	Second Stage	Third Stage

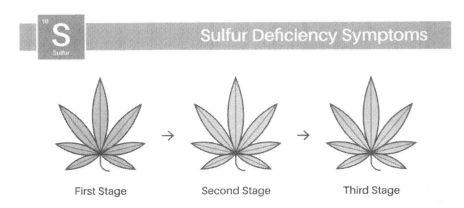

CLOGGED SYSTEM

As discussed previously, algae is a common cause of clogged lines and pumps. If this is the case, follow the instructions above to rid the system of algae.

Lines and pumps can also be clogged if growing medium or plant matter drifts into the lines or blocks drain holes or drip emitters. To avoid this from the start, you can place filter material over any plug or hole in the reservoir or grow tray. If this is a potential issue with your system, the best solution is diligence. Monitor the pumps, drains, and drip lines. Check them daily to make sure they are working properly.

GETTING STARTED

Hydroponic systems are varied in design and complexity, in size and style, yet each one can be built by a home gardener without too much difficulty. There is a lot to bear in mind regarding nutrients, water and pH which you may not have had to pay attention to for soil-based gardening. However, once you've worked with these factors for a little while, it becomes easier. There's always a learning curve when exploring new techniques.

Hydroponic systems are a lot of fun to build and play around with. Once you've gotten comfortable with how they work, you'll be hooked. When you see how productive they are and how little space they take up compared to soil-based systems, you'll be more than pleased. The results will speak for themselves. Start off with one of the simpler systems if you're feeling hesitant and move your way up to the more complicated ones. Feel free to experiment to find out which ones work best for your location and plants. And most of all, have fun!

For those of you who want to dive deeper into practice already, check out the free bonus. Here you'll get some handy tips for the everyday hydroponic gardener on microclimate control, water, nutrients, lighting, and seeding. All you need to do is click the link and download the PDF: https://DIYhydroponics.gr8.com

WHAT DO YOU THINK ABOUT THE BOOK?

First of all, thank you for purchasing this book. I know you could have picked any number of books to read, but you picked this book and for that I am extremely grateful.

If you enjoyed this book and found some benefit in reading this, I'd like to hear from you and hope that you could take some time to post a review on Amazon. Your feedback and support means the world to me and will make this book even better.

If you'd like to leave a review all you need to do is to go to the book's product page on Amazon and click on **"Write a Customer Review"**

I wish you all the best for your hydroponic journey!

APPENDIX I - GLOSSARY

Absorption
The intake of water and other materials through root or leaf cells.

Acid soil
Soil with a pH below 7 on a pH scale of 0 to 14. The lower the pH, the more acidic the soil. See pH.

Aeration
Mechanically loosening or puncturing soil to increase permeability to water and air.

Aeroponics
A variation of hydroponics that involves the misting of plant roots with nutrient solution.

Alkaline
Refers to medium or nutrient solution with a high pH; any pH over 7 is considered alkaline.

Alkaline soil
Soil with a pH above 7 on a pH scale of 0 to 14. The higher the reading, the more alkaline the soil. See pH.

Blight
Rapid, extensive discoloration, wilting, and death of plant tissue.

Bloom booster
Fertilizer high in phosphorus (P) that increases flower yield.

Botrytis
A fungal disease promoted by cool, moist weather. Also known as

gray mold or fruit rot.

Calcium carbonate (CaCO3)
A compound found in limestone, ashes, bones, and shells; the primary component of lime.

Capillary force
The action by which water molecules bind to the surfaces of soil particles and to each other, thus holding water in fine pores against the force of gravity.

Capillary water
Water held in the tiny spaces between soil particles or between plant cells.

Chelate
A complex organic substance that holds micronutrients, usually iron, in a form that plants can absorb.

Chlorophyll
The green pigment in plants. Responsible for absorbing light energy to power photosynthesis.

Chlorosis
An abnormal yellowing of a leaf.

Clay pebble
A growing medium composed of clay that expands on contact with water, forming small round balls.

Closed system
A hydroponic system, such as nutrient film technique (NFT) systems, that recirculates the nutrient solution.

Coco coir
A growing medium composed of ground coconut husks.

Damping-off
A disease caused by many different organisms. In the most conspicuous cases, a seedling's stem collapses at or near the soil surface, and the seedling topples. Another type rots seedlings before they emerge from the soil or causes seeds to decay before germinating.

Defoliation
The unnatural loss of a plant's leaves, generally to the detriment of its health. Can be caused by high winds, excessive heat, drought, frost, chemicals, insects, or disease.

Diatomite
A fine-grained sedimentary rock formed from consolidated diatomaceous earth.

Drip irrigation
A type of irrigation system in which each plant is fed individually with a small drip tube. The flow is regulated by an emitter common to many hydroponic systems.

Deep water culture (DWC)
A hydroponic method in which plant roots are suspended in 8" or more of nutrient-rich, oxygenated water.

Ebb-and-flow
A hydroponic system in which the plants are sub-irrigated periodically and the nutrient solution drains back to a central cistern for subsequent cycles.

Feeder roots

Fine roots and root branches with a large absorbing area (root hairs). Responsible for taking up the majority of a plant's water and nutrients from the soil.

Fertilizer
A natural or synthetic product added to the soil or sprayed on plants to supply nutrients.

Fungicide
Any material capable of killing fungi. Sulfur and copper sulfate are two common mineral fungicides.

Fungus
An organism that lacks chlorophyll, reproduces via spores, and usually has filamentous growth. Examples are molds, yeasts, and mushrooms.

Fusarium
Any of several fungal diseases that afflict plants; commonly called dry rot or wilt.

Germination
The initial sprouting stage of a seed.

Growing medium
Materials that are used in some hydroponic growing methods to support the plant's roots and, sometimes, to hold nutrients.

Herbicide
A chemical used to kill undesirable plants.

Hydroponics
A method of growing plants without soil. Plants are often suspended in water or inert growing media, and nutrients are supplied in dilute

solutions.

Hygrometer
An instrument for measuring relative humidity in the atmosphere.

Hymenoptera
An insect family made up of species having four membranous wings. Includes bees, wasps, sawflies, and ants.

Insecticide
Any material that kills insects. Includes numerous botanical products, both organic and synthetic.

Lime
A rock powder consisting primarily of calcium carbonate. Used to raise soil pH (decrease acidity).

Loam
A soil composed of roughly equal measures of sand, silt, and clay particles.

Macronutrient
The major minerals used by plants in large amounts. These include nitrogen (N), phosphorus (P), potassium (K), sulfur (S), calcium (Ca), and magnesium (Mg).

Micronutrient
A nutrient used by plants in small amounts, less than 1 part per million. Micronutrients include boron, chlorine, copper, iron, manganese, molybdenum, and zinc. Also called trace elements.

Mineral deficiency
When a plant does not receive a sufficient amount of a mineral, it becomes deficient in that mineral. This interferes with the health and

growth of the plant.

Mycelia
Masses of fungal threads (hyphae) that make up the vegetative body of the fungus.

Mycorrhizae
Beneficial fungi that grow alongside and through plant roots, increasing their ability to take up nutrients from the soil.

Nematode
A microscopic roundworm, usually living in the soil. Some feed on plant roots and spread disease. Others benefit plants by acting as parasites for insect pests.

Nutrient film technique (NFT)
A water culture system based upon constant flow of the nutrient solution past the plant roots. NFT uses a thin film of water flowing through the roots to provide adequate moisture and aeration.

Nitrate (NO3-)
A plant-available form of nitrogen contained in many fertilizers and generated in the soil by the breakdown of organic matter. Excess nitrates in soil can leach into groundwater.

Nitrogen (N)
A primary plant nutrient, especially important for foliage and stem growth.

N-P-K
The acronym for the three primary nutrients contained in manure, compost, and fertilizers. The N stands for nitrogen, the P stands for phosphorus, and the K stands for potassium. On a fertilizer label, the N-P-K numbers refer to the percentage of the primary nutrients (by

weight) in the fertilizer. For example, a 5-10-5 fertilizer contains 5% nitrogen, 10% phosphorous, and 5% potassium.

Nutrient
Any substance, especially in the soil, that is essential for and promotes plant growth.

Nutrient solution
The water solution containing all of the essential plant elements in their correct ratios; the basic nutrient supply for plant roots.

Open (non-recirculating) system
A hydroponic system in which the nutrient solution passes only once through the plant roots; the leachate is not collected and returned to a cistern for repeated cycles.

Organic fertilizer
A natural fertilizer material that has undergone little or no processing. Can include plant, animal, or mineral materials.

Organic matter
Any material originating from a living organism (peat moss, plant residue, compost, ground bark, manure, etc.).

Oxygenation
The supplying of oxygen to a solution. Healthy plant growth requires the nutrient solution to be sufficiently oxygenated.

Parasite
Any animal or plant that lives in, or on, another animal or plant and draws nutrients from its host. Parasites are harmful to the host.

Pathogen

Any organism that causes disease. Generally used to describe bacteria, viruses, fungi, nematodes, and parasitic plants.

Peat
A soil-less medium composed of partially decomposed aquatic, marsh, bog, or swamp vegetation.

Peat Mix
A soil-less medium consisting of a mixture of peat, sand, vermiculite, and/or perlite.

Perlite
A soil-less medium made from fired volcanic pumice.

pH
A scale measuring the acidity or alkalinity of a sample. What the pH scale actually measures is the concentration of hydrogen ion ($H+$) present in a given substance. pH values run from 0 (the most acidic value possible) to 14 (the most alkaline value possible). pH values from 0 to 7 indicate acidity, a pH of 7 is considered to be neutral, while pH values from 7 to 14 indicate alkalinity. The scale is logarithmic, thus a difference of 1 pH unit is equal to a 10-fold change in acidity or alkalinity (depending on the direction), a difference of 2 pH units indicates a 100-fold change, and a difference of 3 pH units indicates a 1,000-fold change.

Phosphorous (P)
A primary plant nutrient, especially important for flower production. In fertilizer, usually provided in the form of phosphate (P_2O_5).

Potassium (K)
A primary plant nutrient, especially important for water uptake and sugar synthesis.

Quick-release fertilizer
A fertilizer that contains nutrients in plant-available forms such as ammonium and nitrate.

Relative humidity
The ratio of water vapor in the air to the amount of water vapor the air could hold at the current temperature and pressure.

Reservoir
The container in a hydroponic system which holds nutrient solution in reserve for use.

Rockwool
A substrate used to grow plants hydroponically; an extruded wool-like product. Formed through a process of melting rock, extruding it into threads, and pressing them into loosely woven sheets at high temperatures.

Root
Generally, the underground portion of a plant. It anchors the plant and absorbs water and nutrients.

Seedling
A young plant, shortly after germination.

Selective pesticide
A pesticide that kills or controls only certain kinds of plants or animals.

Slow-release fertilizer
A fertilizer material that must be converted into a plant-available form by soil micro-organisms.

Soil

A natural, biologically active mixture of weathered rock fragments and organic material at the earth's surface.

Soil-less mix
A sterile potting medium consisting of ingredients such as sphagnum peat moss and vermiculite.

Verticillium
Any of several fungal diseases that afflict plants; commonly called wilt.

Water culture
A hydroponic method of plant production by means of suspending the plant roots in a solution of nutrient-rich, oxygenated water.

Wilt
(1) Lack of freshness and the drooping of leaves from a lack of water.
(2) A vascular disease that interrupts a plant's normal uptake and distribution of water.

APPENDIX II – IDEAL PH LEVEL FOR YOUR HYDROPONIC PLANTS

Plant	Heat (Min|Max)	Heat (optimum)	Light (minimum)
Beans	45°F|80°F	75°F	4-6 hours
Beets	32°F|85°F	70°F	4-6 hours
Carrots	32°F|85°F	70°F	4-8 hours
Celery	45°F|70°F	65°F	4-6 hours
Chard	32°F|90°F	70°F	6 hours
Corn	55°F|100°F	85°F	6-8 hours
Cucumber	60°F|95°F	80°F	6-8 hours
Eggplant	60°F|95°F	75°F	4-6 hours
Lettuce	28°F|80°F	60°F-70°F	3-4 hours
Melons	60°F|95°F	85°F	8 hours
Onions	55°F|85°F	65°F	6 hours
Peas	32°F|80°F	70°F	4-6 hours
Peppers	60°F|90°F	75°F	4-8 hours
Potatoes	45°F|80°F	70°F	6-8 hours
Radishes	40°F|85°F	70°F	6 hours
Spinach	28°F|75°F	65°F	3-4 hours
Squash	60°F|90°F	80°F	8 hours
Strawberries	60°F|80°F	75°F	6 hours
Tomatoes	60°F-62°F|95°F	75°F	8 hours
Cabbage family (Broccoli, Cabbage, Cauliflower, Brussels Sprouts, Kohirabi, Kale)	28°F|75°F		4-6 hours

MORE BOOKS ABOUT HYDROPONICS

If you want to know which hydroponic system and crops work best for your personal situation, check out the first book in Richard Bray's book series on Amazon:

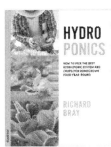

Hydroponics: How to Pick the Best Hydroponic System and Crops for Homegrown Food Year-Round.

In detail, this book allows you to…

Select easy-to-grow herbs, vegetables and fruits and to taste the pleasure of your homegrown food

• See which crops are best suited to each hydroponic system

• Get an overview of which growing mediums work best for each system and plant

Get the most out of your money, time and space by choosing a hydroponic system that suits your needs

• Decide which system suits your own lifestyle by considering your budget, time, space and level of experience

ABOUT THE AUTHOR

Richard's father was a keen gardener and that is where his interest in all natural things began. As a youngster, he enjoyed nothing better than helping his father in the garden. Nowadays, he finds himself at the opposite end of life. Having had a satisfying career, he now has time to potter around in his garden and take care of his small homestead. Much of the food on his dinner table is homegrown. He likes to experiment with various gardening methods and find new ways to grow bountiful crops year-round.

He wants to share his knowledge and show how easy and rewarding it is to set up your own prosperous garden. In his opinion, you don't need a huge budget to get started. When you do get started, you will soon feel, and taste, the benefits of growing your own food.

Learn more about Richard Bray at amazon.com/author/richardbray

Printed in Poland
by Amazon Fulfillment
Poland Sp. z o.o., Wrocław